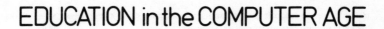

EDUCATION in the COMPUTER AGE

MANAGING INFORMATION
A Series of Books in Organization Studies and Decision-Making

Edited by **AARON WILDAVSKY,** *University of California, Berkeley*

What impact does the computer have on organizations (both public and private), and the individual decision makers within them?

How can "data" be converted into "information for decision"?

Who produces (and who consumes) such data? with what effects? under which conditions?

What are the sources of error—and the means of overcoming them—in contemporary management information system (MIS)?

What is the state of the art in MIS theory?

How can we increase our understanding of information and its management, as well as the surrounding organizational environment?

These are critical questions in an era of information overload, coupled with the need for decision-making by managers and policymakers dealing with finite resources. The **Managing Information** series meets the need for timely and careful analysis of these vital questions. Studies from a variety of disciplines and methodological perspectives will be included. The series will analyze information management from both public and private sectors; empirical as well as theoretical materials will be presented.

STANLEY POGROW

EDUCATION
in the
COMPUTER AGE
issues of policy,
practice,
and reform

Foreword by Michael W. Kirst

Volume 6
MANAGING INFORMATION:
A Series of Books in Organization
Studies and Decision-Making
Series Editor: **AARON WILDAVSKY**

SAGE PUBLICATIONS
Beverly Hills / London / New Delhi

For information address:

SAGE Publications, Inc.
275 South Beverly Drive
Beverly Hills, California 90212

SAGE Publications India Pvt. Ltd.
C-236 Defence Colony
New Delhi 110 024, India

SAGE Publications Ltd
28 Banner Street
London EC1Y 8QE, England

Printed in the United States of America

Library of Congress Cataloging in Publication Data

Pogrow, Stanley.
   Education in the computer age.

   (Managing information ; v. 6)
   Bibliography: p.
   1. Education—United States—Data processing.   2. Computer-assisted instruction—United States.   3. Education—Data processing—Government policy—United States.
I. Title.   II. Series.
LB1028.43.P63   1983   370'.28'5   83-11213
ISBN 0-8039-1992-1

FIRST PRINTING

CONTENTS

To my parents, whose strength has always been a source of inspiration. I know this is not a grandchild, but at least it's something.

LIST OF TABLES

LIST OF FIGURES

ACKNOWLEDGMENTS

This work has been made possible by support provided by many individuals. An opportunity to work for the Policy Research and Analysis group at the National Science Foundation provided the environment in which the initial ideas germinated. Financial support was provided by Joel Sherman of the School Finance Task Force in the National Institute for Education.

The ideas were further nourished by the comments and criticisms of many. I am especially indebted to Aaron Wildavsky for his enthusiasm and support. Comments on early versions of the manuscript were also provided by David Berliner, Larry Hutchens, Gloria Frazier, James Guthrie, Peter Hathaway, Robert Hess, Michael Kirst, Shirley McCune, Douglas Mitchell, Allan Odden, Larry Leslie, and Marc Tucker. Having the opportunity to exchange ideas with these individuals made this a fulfilling venture. Thanks are also in order to the many educators who took time to share ideas and experiences. The author is, however, solely accountable for the final product.

Assistance in the preparation of the manuscript was provided by Fran, Helen and Jesse. A special thanks to Faye who kept everything going in the panicky moments.

FOREWORD

STANLEY POGROW HAS thrown down a major challenge to public education. He proposes to change the most difficult part of the public schooling process—the technical core of instructional methods and activities. He calls for the educational system to transform the classroom through harnessing the computer. Computer technology should not be a mere incremental addition like driver training or filmstrips. But this will be no easy task, and his tone reflects a mixture of anxiety and prescriptive advice on specific implementation strategies. He wants schools to teach *through* technology rather than just *about* technology.

Recent large-scale studies by Cuban and Goodlad reach the overwhelming conclusion that there has been amazingly little change in instructional methods or use of technology over the past forty years.

At all levels of schooling, a very few teaching procedures—explaining or lecturing, monitoring seatwork and quizzing—accounted for most all those we observed in our sample of 1,016 classrooms. Teachers varied in the quality of their lecturing, but "teacher talk" was by far the dominant classroom activity. Teachers rarely encouraged student-to-student dialog or provided opportunities for students to work collaboratively or to plan, set goals . . . and the like.[1]

In his study of high schools since 1900, Cuban (1982) stresses that it is "a remarkably invulnerable institution" with a durable structure.[2] Reformers can add things to the structure, like school lunch and vocational education, but changes in the basic pattern are rare. These studies seem to confirm Pogrow's prediction that environmental pressure on schools from computer technology and the information society will confront stiff institutional resistance. Computers may merely be incremental, adding an extra department in the secondary school (e.g., driver education), or a supplemental enrichment device like classroom TV.

But at this point Pogrow's analysis transcends the usual skepticism. He presents a strong case on: (1) why the schools must adapt fundamentally to computers or suffer greatly and (2) how to prevent undesirable public school resistance through specific strategies and tactics that are quite feasible. On the latter point, he proposes low-cost approaches for bringing in computers to teach the higher-order skills of synthesis, analysis, and math problem solving.

Schools rarely incorporate lasting changes unless there is a strong internal or external constituency for maintenance of the new initiative. These constituencies have usually formed around structural additions that can be easily monitored. The addition of vocational education or music did not require a large change in teaching methods or classroom activities in the traditional subjects of math or English. Moreover, vocational education has a powerful constituency, including labor, business, and agriculture. Where is the constituency for the nontraditional delivery system using computers in the regular classroom for core subjects? Here is where Pogrow's idea of "environmental collapse" comes in. He sketches an economic transformation including widespread office automation and computers in the home. He hopes that the school will not resist this dual pincer movement of computers in the home and the workplace. If it does, public education may be abandoned by more people who seek private alternatives ranging from schools to home-based technology education. But if one does not agree that massive changes in the home and workplace will be galvanized by the new technology, then the environmental collapse notion becomes much less compelling. Or one could agree on these large external changes but still contend that they will *not* result in a focused school constituency for nontraditional technology.

The primary significance of the book does not lie in its warning that education may have to adapt to massive environmental pressures in this decade, or in simplistic advocacy, but rather in its development of a comprehensive policy agenda at local, state, and federal levels for facilitating such adaptation. Many of the quick-fix initiatives currently being touted as necessary for enabling schools to cope with the information age are judged to be inappropriate, while other proposals to buy more of the traditional coping tactics are judged to be inadequate. Pogrow supports his judgments with an impressive array of social scientific evidence from a variety of disciplines, culminating in a series of alternative, fascinating, and often counter-intuitive recommendations.

The implications of these proposals for reorienting the research priorities of a number of disciplines are as innovative as the policy recommendations themselves. Pogrow argues that it is possible to anticipate and enact the R&D needed to support the recommended nontraditional initiatives in time to meet intensified demands for change. Scholars and funding agencies will, of course, find these research recommendations to be important and thought-provoking.

The tone of the volume is supportive of the goals of institutionalized public schooling. Pogrow believes that the schools can adapt to the information age. Moreover, he suggests numerous ways to do this without starting over and redesigning the functions of schools.

This is not a book arguing that technology will eliminate teachers, create teacher-proof curriculum, or result in vast cost-savings. The analysis stresses that teachers are still vital and computer-based technology will leverage available expertise, provide students with independent learning, and stimulate learning of higher-order skills. The presentation should not frighten unions concerned about losing jobs, but it challenges educators to revamp drastically their use of technology and teaching styles, methods, and activities.

The book is a how-to-do-it manual as well as an eloquent argument for a new strategy. Some chapters focus on everything from specific instructional techniques, to buying hardware or software, to policy issues at the state or even nation level. Despite this impressive practical advice, however, the author's concluding chapter is a rather emotional plea for more than disjointed incremental adaptation to the computer age. He charges and impressively supports the notions that events have overrun the capabilities of the existing school instructional delivery systems. Change is essential for survival of public schools. Unfortunately, the school response to date has been to "simply grasp obvious straws" like differential pay or industry school "partnerships," or to use "computer literacy" as only a short-term attempt to wall off the core instructional process in the basic subjects from nontraditional computer-based delivery systems.

After reading and thinking about this intriguing volume, I am still unsure whether environmental collapse will force the schools to a nonincremental response. The patterns and methods of instruction have persisted for fifty years, and it may be another fifty before we see much change. New technology has not made many inroads into school policy since the blackboard and moveable desk. It remains to be seen whether the computer will have the same impact as Gutenberg's press on the basic means of delivering instruction. But if, as a principal or superintendant, I wanted to adjust my school to computers, I would find the advice and concepts in this book essential. Similarly, if I were in a position to help restructure state or federal policy mandates, I would treat this book as my map. There should be enough change-oriented people to ensure a wide readership for this novel book. Despite the rapid changes in microcomputer-technology, Pogrow's concepts will have a long life. There is something in here for almost every interest in this burgeoning field.

—Michael W. Kirst

NOTES

1. John I. Goodlad, "A Study of Schooling," *Phi Delta Kappan,* 64 (April 1983), p. 552.
2. Larry Cuban, "Persistent Instruction," *Phi Delta Kappan,* 64 (October 1982), pp. 113-118.

INTRODUCTION

THIS IS NOT a book about technology per se. Rather, it is a book about a traditional goal—improving education. What is not traditional is the context in which this goal needs to be pursued: *We must improve our schools in the context of constrained resources and in the midst of massive environmental changes,* both in our economy and in the way work is performed. Today's tight resources make school improvement difficult under any circumstances. The environmental technology changes magnify the difficulty by creating the need both to improve and to expand educational services. Not only must the delivery of traditional skills be improved, but the curriculum must be expanded to include new skills that schools have either traditionally ignored or never succeeded at providing to the vast majority of students. What policies and practices are needed if education is to cope successfully with this dual pressure, and what role must the new computer-based technology play in these strategies?

Developing policies to enable education to cope with these pressures requires a bridging of the gap between technologists who view the use of technology as an inherently valuable end and traditionalists who seek the ends of school improvement but rely on techniques that, by themselves, are unlikely to be viable in the emergent context of environmental change. Integrating these two perspectives is difficult, given the traditional dichotomy between them.

Concern about the potential use and impact of technology in education has largely been the domain of a small group of people who work in areas such as computer-assisted instruction (CAI) and artificial intelligence.* The work of these technologists has been essen-

---

*The term "technology" as used throughout this book, unless otherwise specified, will refer to programmable computer-based systems. This includes computers and devices that depend on computers for their operation, such as robots and telecommunication equipment.

tially peripheral to the major traditions of educational thought and practice. Technology issues have also been largely ignored by traditional scholarly disciplines, such as political science, sociology, and finance, which have provided much of the intellectual fuel for educational policy during the past two decades. One consequence of this bifurcation is that existing work on technology in education is simplistic from a policy perspective, consisting largely of attempts to describe technological capabilities or to define computer literacy.

Technologists have occasionally exerted some influence on educational practice (as they did with disastrous consequences in the late sixties) and have participated in policy deliberations about education (as occurred during the 1979-80 hearings by George Brown's House Subcommittee on Science, Research and Technology). Aside from the occasional instances just cited, however, research on the development and impact of technology in schools and society has been essentially segregated from the intellectual traditions of education and much of the social sciences. Most educators and social scientists tend to consider themselves lay people when it comes to technology.

Social scientists do, of course, use computers to analyze their data, but they seldom collect data about how the computer affects social systems. Information about technology is published in technical journals, which are usually not read by educational practitioners or social scientists. One rarely finds articles about computers in the *Harvard Educational Review* or the *American Political Science Review,* for example.

Nor have educators traditionally paid much attention to technology concerns. Recent assessments of the impact of changing technology on education, such as the joint National Science Foundation-Department of Education (1980) study and research by Nilles et al. (1980) and Walling, Thomas, and Larson (1979), have been ignored by educators and educational publications. Prior to 1982, there were virtually no articles in practitioner-oriented school administration journals about computers, despite the fact that most school administrators rely extensively on computer-based management systems. Policy groups that assess the social impact of technology tend to be housed in business or engineering schools rather than colleges of liberal arts and sciences or schools of public administration. Departments of technology in colleges of education still tend to focus on training teachers how to operate old (in a technological sense) machines, such as movie projectors.

The intellectual split between those who study the implications of technological development and those who are concerned with the generation of social science theory is largely a result of the different backgrounds, language systems, and interests of each group. It is rare that these cultural differences are bridged. A notable recent example of successful integration of these cultures is Seymour Papert's (1980) book *Mindstorms*. Mindstorms talks about technology from the perspectives of learning theory and anthropology, focusing on the world of children instead of engineering issues.

The lack of integration between technology and educational policy analysis was of little consequence under the conditions that prevailed during the sixties and seventies. Although a number of significant scientific breakthroughs occurred in physics and biology labs, the technologies that were relevant to everyday life underwent slow evolutionary change and contained no real surprises or new opportunities for education. (*Sesame Street* was an exception). Cars got better, but everyone still drove to work at pretty much the same speed. The eighties, however, appears to be one of those rare periods when revolutionary new technologies emerge that present opportunities, and compelling economic incentives, to change the way work is performed.

Not since the beginning of the industrial revolution, when the compelling economics of the factory overwhelmed the political arrangements that had reinforced the preeminence of the craft guilds and the urban lifestyle replaced the rural one, have there been such powerful new technological alternatives and fiscal incentives for modifying the routines of everyday life. Under such conditions, failure to integrate technological issues with educational policy and social science theory can result in misdirected policy initiatives that are based on outdated precedents and social science theories that ignore the real-time structural changes occurring in society. Social scientists rarely have the opportunity to study economic revolutions in real time, and it would be unfortunate if such an opportunity were lost because of existing scholarly traditions.

This book has three main objectives. The first is to establish a framework for viewing educational needs and change primarily within the context of social technological change, and to synthesize the research and policy implications of such a perspective. The second objective is to provide policymakers and educators *useful* guidance in preparing for, and dealing with, the educational issues and possibilities that changing technology will effect during this decade. The third objective is to bring technological concerns into the mainstream of general educational thought and practice by demonstrating the intellectual importance and pragmatic necessity of such integration. Adapting to new technological realities is the most important policy issue facing public education during this decade if it is to avoid emerging into the 1990s as a vestige of an economic order that has been supplanted and as homage to political power structures that no longer retain their former degree of control.

If this book is to suggest ways of adapting to changing circumstances, it needs to project the future and its consequences—specifically. Simply talking about future alternatives, while protecting the author against the possibility of being wrong, does not suit the criterion of usefulness. The need for at least some degree of precision in the estimates dictated the methodological approach that was selected.

2. DESCRIPTION OF THE METHODOLOGY

A review of existing policy work in educational technology reveals two main problems. First, much of the work (e.g., Kincaid, McEachron, & McKinney, 1974; Levin & Woo, 1980) focuses on the cost-effectiveness of using technology in education at only a single point in time—usually the present. To the extent that it takes time for policy interventions to affect the educational system, or that the cost-effectiveness potential increases under newer anticipatable forms of technology, a single-point-in-time analysis is inadequate under conditions of evolving technology.

A second limitation of existing methodology is the tendency to make generalizations about the role and use of technology based on a single factor while ignoring potentially countervailing effects. The most common factor analyzed is whether technology will improve learning effectiveness, or whether educators will willingly adopt technology. Such analysis tends to treat the use of technology as an internally initiated innovation opportunity. These studies inevitably conclude, on the basis of precedent, that schools will not adopt technology, since large institutions seldom voluntarily innovate in the absence of strong external pressures to change. Such analyses ignore that conditions for massive environmental technological change exist *now,* and that external pressures are already being felt.

In order to avoid these problems, a methodology is required that (a) takes a longitudinal perspective, (b) examines the interactive effects of a variety of key factors, and (c) views technological adoption from the perspective of pressures generated in a given organization's environment. With respect to the latter, there appear to be two kinds of environmental or societal factors. The first are *general* factors, such as the overall state of the economy in the world and the United States. *Specific* environmental factors also influence an organization's adoption decision, such as the extent to which the given technology is adopted by competitors and clients. In this book, presenting alternative scenarios for each type of environmental factor would have resulted in too many scenarios with too tenuous a link to educational policy. As a result, it was decided to use the single, most likely, scenario for the general economic factors: slow to moderate growth of the economy throughout the decade, assuming no cataclysmic events such as a world war, a major energy shortage, or a major reduction in world trade resulting from economic protectionism.

Adopting a high-probability perspective for the general environmental conditions has the added advantage of eliminating the need for multiple scenarios of the specific environmental factors. That is, under conditions of relatively stable, even slow, growth, it appears that societal utilization of technology will follow a "relatively" predictable series of phases (which will be described in Chapter I) that are driven largely by economic factors. As a result, it was decided to use *technology events* rather than multiple scenarios. A technology event is defined as a particular evolutionary phase in societal utilization of technology.

The basic methodology of this study is to describe time frames for technology events (TEs) that can be expected to affect the external environment of schools in specific ways during this decade. Consequences of each TE will be derived (where possible) for each of the following variables:

(a) educational needs (EN),
(b) educational demands (ED), and
(c) technological opportunity (TO) for alternative forms of educational delivery systems and political dynamics.

This relationship can be expressed mathematically as:

$$TE_i \rightarrow EN_i, ED_i, TO_i \qquad [1]$$

The projected impacts of each TE will be explored to determine their policy implications for education. Even if the predicted time spans for TEs turn out to be somewhat inaccurate, the concept is still useful since it provides a benchmark against which to adjust the time frames for the policy concerns generated by the functional consequences of equation 1.

While the variables in equation 1 can be viewed as linked by elements of economic determinism and thereby subject to forces that are at least partly rational (hence predictable), the response of the public school system to the impact of environmental TEs, on the other hand, cannot be viewed as necessarily rational or systematically related to anything predictable. As a result, instead of trying to predict the likely responses of the public school system, this book will explore research issues associated with determining what an appropriate response would be given the expected TEs, and the policy issues associated with removing traditional constraints to such adaptation.

Defining what constitutes an appropriate response by schools to projected TEs is as important as predicting the TEs. Unfortunately, the tradition of isolating technology use from contemporary educational thought is likely to lead to a perception that the solution to the issues raised by environmental technological change requires a series of add-on policies that are divorced from the mainstream of ongoing educational issues and problems. This tendency is already reflected in the computer literacy movement, which often views the addition of several curriculum units on technological awareness as an appropriate response to increasing societal use of technology.

Rather than viewing the educational issues raised by changing technology as separate ones, the emphasis in this book is to view the problem as one of general curricular reform under conditions of constrained resources. Social science research will be used to develop a conceptual framework for determining what constitutes an appropriate curricular response by school districts to projected TEs, as well as for designing delivery systems to overcome impediments to such response. The primary policy focus is to determine which of the existing constraints on appropriate school response can be eliminated by initiatives at the state and federal levels. The major policy goal is to create greater opportunity for those schools and states that wish to adapt to changing environmental needs to do so. Recommendations will be made for specific policy initiatives, and their implications for the practice of education will be explored. Given existing fiscal realities, policies that can be implemented at relatively low cost will be emphasized.

1. OVERVIEW OF THE CHAPTERS

The first half of this book parallels the relationship between the variables in equation 1. Chapter I contains a technology assessment that describes the nature of the technology events during this decade. Chapter II discusses the implications of the environmental TEs for changing the nature of educational needs and the types of educational services demanded by the public. Chapter III examines the impact of TEs on the evolution of technological opportunity and discusses its implications for developing new forms of delivery systems. The limitations of existing delivery systems in relation to the potential of the new forms is also discussed. Chapter IV examines some of the impediments to appropriate use of technology in education and speculates on the political consequences if public schools do not respond adequately to the projected environmental press for technological change.

The second part of the book focuses on deriving recommendations for policy and practice. Chapter V provides a framework for determining what an appropriate response on the part of schools to the changing environment would/should be. This chapter discusses what constitutes "appropriate" uses of computers that educators and policymakers should/must strive to achieve, for both instructional and administrative applications. Chapters VI and VII discuss policy issues at the federal and state levels that must be resolved if existing impediments to an appropriate response to environmental demands for more technologically relevant curricula are to be eliminated. Chapter VI focuses on policy issues that must be resolved at the national level; Chapter VII on those that are regional. Chapter VIII summarizes the implications of the policy and research recommendations in the preceding chapters for educational practice and professional training.

ASSESSING ENVIRONMENTAL TECHNOLOGICAL CHANGE

HISTORICALLY, FAR MORE technologies and re-
form ideas have been proposed and available for use in the public
schools than have actually been adopted on a wide-scale basis. Educational television, teaching machines, and new math are examples of
technologies and proposed reforms that, despite aggressive advocates, had little impact on schools. Examples of technologies that did
influence the instructional process in public schools are books and
components of vocational education. Why do so few of the available
technologies affect education, and what particular set of conditions
determines whether they will be adopted?

In examining this question, Kirst, Tyack, & Hansot (1979) came
to the conclusion that innovations persist if they meet the following
criteria:

(a) The innovation creates an extra layer of structure.
(b) The innovation is easily monitored.
(c) A political constituency emerges to support it.

While these attributes are sufficient to explain innovations that are
added on to an existing structure, such as school lunch programs, or
that simplify the management of the existing structure, such as report
cards or the Carnegie Unit, they do little to explain innovations in the

21

operation of the core of the organization. In other words, the foregoing criteria do not (by the admission of the authors) explain why some instructional innovations (i.e., changes in course content or methodology) are adopted but most are not. The criteria do not by themselves explain why an instructional technology such as the book is institutionalized, whereas instructional television, new math, and programmed instruction are not.

The only hypothesis that seems to explain instructional technology adoption decisions over the centuries is that technologies have a major impact on instruction only if they meet both of the following criteria:

(a) The technology is a cultural one (i.e., it is found in a large number of homes).
(b) The technology is a primary work tool.

The former factor reduces the tendency of parents and the general public to oppose the introduction of a given technology into the schools; the latter generates a demand from the public to adopt the technology and provide training in its use.

This chapter contains a technology assessment of the extent to which microcomputers are likely to become a cultural technology and a primary work tool. A *cultural technology* is defined as one that is found in at least 10 percent of households. It is at this point that a technology is sufficiently widespread that its use is not limited to some highly specialized subgroup. A *primary work tool* is defined as a technology that transforms the nature of work (which excludes coffee pots and calculators) and whose use is required for 25 percent of jobs in society.

The basic working hypothesis of this book is that *the greater the extent to which microcomputers become both a cultural and a work-tool technology, the greater will be the demand and need for their use in schools.* The goal of the technology assessment in this chapter is to describe different phases and degrees of microcomputer use in the environment in terms of technology events. Of particular concern is determining the point when environmental use of technology will reach levels that constitute cultural acceptance (10 percent of households) and a primary work tool (25 percent of jobs).

1. LIMITS OF
TECHNOLOGY ASSESSMENT METHODOLOGIES

Technology assessment (TA) is far from an exact science. The basic methodology of TA consists of interviewing "those in the know" to gather data about the basic independent variables, which are then plugged into utility functions that have described the rate of adoption of "similar" types of innovations in the past. In addition to the obvious limitations of such methodology, the definition of TA is ambiguous. TA is used to represent a number of different analyses such as

(a) assessing the rate of growth of technological capability;
(b) assessing the rate of adoption in society of the technological capability; and
(c) assessing the social consequences of different rates of adoption of new technology.

These different types of TA form a continuum of analytic ambiguity in which the validity of projections declines as one moves from a type a to a type c analysis. For example, Moore's Law, that the amount of circuitry that can be put on a chip of given size doubles each year, has been a remarkably accurate type a predictor over the past several decades. Type b analyses, on the other hand, have been spotty in their accuracy. Assessments have consistently underestimated the use of microcomputers and overestimated the acceptance of teleconferencing and electronic fund transfer applications. The risk analysis program at the National Science Foundation represents an attempt to develop methodological conventions for incorporating type c analyses into formal policy debates, but there has been little success to date in anticipating the social consequences of new technology. Nevertheless, type c analyses are the most critical for social scientists and policymakers. With these cautions in mind, an effort will be made to synthesize and evaluate the TA literature that focuses on small computers and their progenies: robots, office automation, new forms of telecommunications, and information utilities and data base services. Where possible, tentative estimates of type c effects will be made.

2. THE GROWING CAPABILITY
OF COMPUTER TECHNOLOGY

The following statement by Robert Noyce (1977), chairman of Intel Corporation, best summarizes the practical consequence of Moore's Law in the recent past:

> Today's microcomputer, at a cost of perhaps $300, has more computing capacity than the first large electronic computer, ENIAC. It is 20 times faster, has a larger memory, is thousands of times more reliable, consumes the power of a lightbulb rather than that of a locomotive, occupies 1/30,000 the volume and costs 1/10,000 as much. (p. 65)

If Moore's Law continues to operate, then it will be possible to put today's most powerful computers on a chip by the end of this decade. While there is no guarantee that the law will continue to operate, the Department of Defense's Very High-Scale Integration Circuitry (VHSIC) program, and several intensive research and development efforts in other countries, suggest that it probably will. Several companies have already announced minicomputers on a chip, and the Japanese have announced that they will be producing a memory chip (256 Kb) that contains four times the capacity of existing chips by the end of 1983. There does not appear to be any slowing down in the operation of Moore's Law.

The semiconductor industry, which manufactures the electronic chips, is the most productive one in the United States today. Its productivity is estimated to have increased 20,000 times during the past two decades. The total worldwide market for semiconductor products is estimated to grow from $13 billion to $60 billion during this decade (Nilles, 1980, pp. 6-17). As a result of increasing productivity and demand, the cost of computing has declined rapidly. Licklider (1980) has noted that the amount of information processing that can be done per unit time by one dollar's worth of computer hardware has doubled approximately every two years since 1943, and has been doubling every fifteen months since 1965. Noyce (1977) has predicted that the cost of computing per function will continue to decline at a rate of 25 percent per year through 1986.

The use of computers is extremely price-elastic in that as the cost declines, use increases. The major cost reductions cited above have made it possible to produce low-cost computers, one of which now sells for only $100. As the price of computers has fallen, the size of the economic unit that can afford them has likewise shrunk, and the number of tasks to which they can be applied has increased. Computer processors have now become so inexpensive that they are replacing mechanical components that perform measuring and controlling functions in a wide range of equipment, from sewing machines to airplanes. Such replacement not only reduces costs but also enables the functioning of the equipment to be changed via software modifications as opposed to expensive retooling.

The growing pervasiveness of these small computers is enhanced by the fact that all modern telecommunications and information handling systems are based on the electronic generation, transmission, storage, reception, and utilization of digital information. Virtually identical combinations of processors, memories, and input/output devices can be programmed to function as telecommunications, data processing, or work processing systems (Kalba & Jakimo, 1980).

As the capabilities of small, inexpensive computers increase (some new ones have the capabilities of existing minicomputers), it is becoming possible to use them to simulate many of the human senses. Progress is being made in using digital information to represent vision, hearing, touch, and even some aspects of intelligence itself. It is expected that most of the technical problems in having low-cost computers perform these functions will be solved by the early 1990s. Primitive (limited-vocabulary) voice input devices and speech synthesizers are already available for less than $400.

The decreasing cost of computers is also creating mass markets for what were previously highly exotic applications that were available only on very expensive systems of limited affordability. One example is computer-aided design (CAD) techniques, which make it possible to develop and test prototype designs on the computer without having to make physical models. Another example is computer-aided manufacturing (CAM), wherein computers control assembly line machines. Space exploration led to the development of digital techniques

that provided recorded pictures and audio superior to those of traditional analog techniques. These capabilities are becoming available to
consumers in the form of a whole new generation of digital home
stereo and video systems. In addition, highly sophisticated graphics
capabilities are becoming available in inexpensive computers.

As a result of all these existing and developing capabilities, computers are not only affecting computing; they are also changing the
way we work and play, and even the economy itself. Computers and
the devices they control are, therefore, going to have an increasing role
in determining how we live. The next several sections will give brief
descriptions of these new devices, along with assessments (where possible) of their rate of adoption in the home and workplace.

3. RATE OF ADOPTION OF
MICROCOMPUTERS AND
INTELLIGENT VIDEO DISK SYSTEMS

Business Week (August 17, 1981) estimates computers to be a $62
billion business. The U.S. General Accounting Office estimates that
the federal government alone spends about $20 billion a year for com-
puters, software, and related services. The computer bill for top Fortune 500 companies can exceed $100 million annually. Most of these
costs, however, represent investments in large computers. The trend
that is of most concern to education is the growth of the smaller computers, since most schools, homes, and businesses that computerize
during this decade will use such computers. Small computers are usually referred to as either microcomputers (micros) or personal computers. (The most commonly available microcomputers at this time,
such as Apple and TRS-80, are 8-bit micros. The IBM personal computer is an example of the new 16-bit systems, which are eight to ten
times more powerful than the 8-bit micros. Hewlett Packard and Intel
have announced even more powerful, 32-bit, processor chips. These
latter systems will provide the capability to pack the computing power
of a room-sized powerful mini into a desktop system.)

Nilles et al. (1980) have done the most careful assessment to date of the growth of personal computers. (These estimates refer only to pro-grammable devices and do not include electronic game machines or microprocessors in appliances.) They used two forecasting models: one with optimistic (high) assumptions about growth, the other with pessimistic (low) ones. In addition, a Delphi panel was convened to estimate the growth of personal computers. The results of this study are displayed in Table 1.

The range of estimates in Table 1 is quite high (a 3.5:1 ratio be-tween the high and low estimates). It is, however, significant that an extensive penetration into the home is projected. According to the high projection, there will be sufficient cumulative sales to first-time buyers by 1990 that almost half the expected 85 million households in this country will have a computer. A more recent study by the Yankee Group (1982) predicts that the number of computers in homes could reach 35 to 50 million by the end of the decade.

There are a number of reasons to adopt the more optimistic esti-mates of the foregoing projections. First, there is the historic tendency to underestimate the growth of the microcomputer market. The sec-ond reason for optimism is that prices are falling more rapidly than anticipated. The $600 Commodore 64 micro introduced a price-per-

TABLE 1   Projections of Microcomputer Sales by Market

	Annual Units Sold (thousands)			Cumulative Units Sold (thousands)	
	1978	1985	1990	1985	1990
USC High					
Consumer	170	3,050	8,803	7,610	39,083
Education	15	250	538	650	2,875
Office	40	788	3,450	1,865	11,848
Total	255	4,088	12,800	10,225	55,800
Delphi Panel	255	1,600	5,200	5,800	23,000
USC Low					
Consumer	125	882	2,424	3,070	11,092
Education	15	74	150	304	886
Office	85	350	604	1,587	4,041
Total	225	1,306	3,178	4,961	15,999

SOURCE: Nilles et al. (1980), pp. 3-16

formance capability in 1982 that had not previously been expected to be available until 1985. (In 1983 it is being widely sold for as little as $350.) The introduction of the under-$100 Timex computer in 1982 forced all other vendors to discount their systems aggressively. (Timex expects eventually to sell more computers than watches.) As vendors become more aware of the price elasticity of computer sales and more systems (particularly Japanese) enter the marketplace, there will be increasing downward pressure on prices, which will stimulate over-all sales.

Indeed, recent sales data suggest that the pace of sales is accelerating faster than the pessimistic and Delphi projections of the Nilles et al. (1980) study. According to Blundell (1983) and Friedrich (1983), the estimates of the Delphi projection for total sales of 1.6 million units by 1985 were approached or exceeded by actual 1982 figures. The former study predicts an elevenfold increase in total sales between 1981 and 1991. Preliminary results suggest that 1983 sales are continuing to accelerate beyond previous expectations. This suggests that the true rate of growth will approach the optimistic projections of the Nilles study, for the home as well as the office.

Perhaps the most important reason to be optimistic about the growth in home computer sales is the phenomenon of the home video game machine. The penetration of these machines into the home has been remarkable. Nulty (1982) reports that the sale of the machines and cartridges reached almost $4 billion in 1982, a fourfold increase since 1980. Landro (1982) reports that as of 1982, 10 percent of U.S. homes had these machines, and that figure is expected to grow to 50 percent by 1985. These machines (specifically, the versions that existed prior to 1983) are not considered computers, since they are not programmable and have evolved, in terms of uses and as a market, separately from home computers. What is significant is that several of the game-machine vendors have announced plans to offer attachments that will convert the machines to computers. It is fairly reasonable to assume that significant numbers of parents will decide to increase the value of their initial investment in the machines to provide educational as well as entertainment opportunities. Given the large number of systems out there, the conversion of home game machines to computers could result in a massive increase in the number of home computers that would exceed even the optimistic assumptions of the Nilles (1980) study.

For these reasons, it seems appropriate to be fairly optimistic in projecting the penetration of computers into the home. Therefore, the estimate adopted for the purposes of this work is that 35 to 40 percent of households will have computers by the end of this decade. This figure represents an estimate between the high and the Delphi projections of the Nilles et al. study, which is weighted toward the upper end. In addition, as many as 10 percent of households will probably have computers by around 1985. What this means is that by the end of the decade the computer will have become a cultural technology for the middle class as well as the rich. The trend toward adoption of microcomputers by the middle class will be well under way by mid-decade.

The evidence of increasing popular enthusiasm for acquiring and using computers is also substantiated by the public's growing interest in obtaining information about computers. *Business Week* (August 17, 1981) notes that in the last three years, twelve new computer journals (mostly for the non-computer scientist) were established and that advertising revenues for the ten largest computing journals were up 50 percent from the previous year's levels. The number of new publications is continuing to increase, and the number of computer user clubs and computer workshops is mushrooming across the nation. The number of stores selling computers (excluding Radio Shack) increased from 2,000 in 1981 to between 10,000 and 15,000 by the end of 1982 (Yankee Group, 1982). The Nilles et al. study estimated that the number of programmers will grow from 5 to 21 million during this decade—a rate that heralds a cultural revolution. This revolution was officially consecrated when *Time* magazine voted the computer 1982's "man of the year."

While the educational potential of the microcomputer is very high, the potential of the computer-controlled video disk system (the intelligent video disk) is even greater. The video disk component adds the capability to store large amounts of data (54,000 frames or pages on a single disk—enough to store the *Encyclopaedia Britannica*), and it can store still and motion pictures, text, data, and sound on the same disk.

These different media are all stored in digital form and can be interspersed and selectively retrieved under computer control. The system can be programmed to use greater amounts of sound and pictures to instruct slow readers, and greater reliance on text for fast readers. Lipson (1980) provides a more complete description of the educational potential of the intelligent video disk. Molnar (1979) estimates that these devices should be available for about $1200 by mid-decade. Brittner, Chen, and Lientz (1981) cite industry projections that 400,000 regular video disk units will be in operation by 1982.

The future use of intelligent video disk systems, which has tremendous potential for education, will be a function of cost and the extent to which software that can take advantage of the capabilities of this technology becomes available.

4. THE GROWING USE OF ROBOTS

One application of computers that is going to have major impact on the labor force is robots. Whether or not one understands that robots are "reprogrammable multifunctional manipulators designed to move parts, tools, or devices through variable programmed motions for the performance of a variety of tasks," it is clear that their use is going to accelerate during the eighties. According to Froehlich (1981), the Robot Institute of America conservatively predicts that the market for robots will grow from $68 million to $210 million during 1980-85. Bylinsky (1979) estimates that sales could grow to between $700 million and $2 billion by 1990. Although only 3,500 robots were sold in the past two decades, 1850 were sold in 1980, and an article in *Business Week* (June 9, 1980) estimates that annual sales will increase to between 23,000 and 200,000 robots by 1990, depending on how many additional companies enter the market. The same article reports that General Electric is planning to increase its robot force from 2 in 1979 to 1,000 in the late eighties, in a move that may replace nearly 37,000 assembly workers.

What is the likely impact on workers? A new, more sophisticated generation of robots that see, feel, and think is reaching maturity in the labs and should be available in the marketplace in three to five years. *Business Week* (June 9, 1980) quotes automation experts as saying that these machines could displace *at least* 65 to 75 percent of today's labor force (although no date is given for this anticipated displacement). Friedrich (1980) cites a forecast by the American Society of Manufacturing Engineers and the University of Michigan that by 1988, 50 percent of the labor in small-component assembly will be replaced by automation. A recent study by Carnegie-Mellon, cited in the same *Business Week* article, contains a more conservative displacement projection and estimates maximum worker displacement at only 7 million factory jobs (or about 25 percent of the total). It is expected that it will take until the year 2000 to displace the first 4 million, but the study suggests that it is impossible to predict the rate of introduction.

While it may be difficult to predict the exact number of displaced workers, Peter Drucker (1980) refers to the shift from blue-collar worker to robot as inevitable. Drucker even suggests that such a shift is necessary, since the number of new workers available to enter the blue-collar labor force will decline rapidly in the future. Drucker likens robots to the fractional horsepower motor that transformed industrial processes a hundred years ago. It does appear, however, that the shift away from blue-collar work will be sufficiently rapid that the skilled machinist of 1990-95 may be as employable as the migrant farm worker is today.

5. THE IMPACT OF TELECOMMUNICATIONS

Telecommunications is a major growth industry whose continued technological development is a key determinant of how rapidly and in what form the technology applications discussed in the following sections will evolve. Jonscher (1981) notes that while all business activity (in constant dollars) had a 30 percent cumulative increase during the previous decade, business use of telecommunications increased 95 percent. The revenues of telecommunication services industries are expected to increase from $54 billion in 1980 to $66.6 billion in 1983.

With new telecommunication services expected to become available in the early to middle eighties, combined with the availability of office automation equipment, AT & T estimates that 75 percent of the $200 billion spent by business for communication in 1978 could be converted to telecommunication-based electronic services, which means a potential market of $150 to $240 billion (in 1978 dollars) by the middle of this decade.

This huge market potential explains why AT & T (with their ACS service) and IBM, along with COMSAT and Aetna (SBS), are investing hundreds of millions of dollars to offer worldwide telecommunications services. As large a company as Xerox had to drop out of the competition when it decided to shelve its XTEN system; it will limit its involvement to local-area office communication systems.

The new telecommunication systems under development will use satellites, earth stations, digital networks, fiber optic telephone cables, microwaves, and/or coaxial cables. All these technologies provide the capability (usually referred to as "wideband" communications) to transmit data at rates in excess of 56,000 bits/second, as opposed to the most commonly used speeds of 300-1,200 bits/second over conventional telephone lines.

In addition to high transmission speed, satellites have the advantage of making distance irrelevant as a factor in communication costs, while coaxial cable provides the potential for two-way communication. Low-energy satellite stations offer the potential of a large increase in the number of frequencies available for satellite transmission. With the cost of the earth stations that receive the satellite signals expected to drop as low as $10,000 in the near future, satellite transmission potentially offers compelling savings over postal or regular telephone service. The Yankee Group (1979) estimated that the cost of sending a 250-word letter in 1985 would have been as low as five to six cents with the projected XTEN service. Such savings can translate into enormous profits for business. American Satellite was the first company to demonstrate, in 1982, that it is possible to earn a profit strictly from selling satellite-based telecommunication services to industry.

6. OFFICE AUTOMATION

Office automation is to white-collar work what robots are to blue-collar work. Data and information are the most rapidly growing resources in organizations, and their management, acquisition, generation, distribution, and analysis are costly, inefficient, and undercapitalized. The number of white-collar workers in this country increased nearly 100 percent between 1954 and 1974 (Yankee Group, 1979). By 1975, white-collar workers constituted a larger percentage of the labor force than blue-collar workers (Giuliano, 1982). By 1980, 60 percent of the $1.3 trillion paid out for wages, salaries, and benefits went to office workers (Uttal, 1982).

The increase in the number of white-collar workers and the fact that each inquiry from a white-collar worker triggers as many as forty other messages in an organization (Strassman, 1980) mean that there has been a hypergeometric increase in the amount of information processed in organizations and in society as a whole. In 1975, the average white-collar employee handled 11 pages of text per day, a statistic that is expected to grow to 15 by 1990. The average amount of information that each employee needs to maintain is increasing from former level of four file drawers at the start of the decade at the rate of 4,000 documents per employee year (Yankee Group, 1979). It appears, however, that this massive amount of costly office work is done in a highly inefficient manner. Strassman (1979) notes that the average office worker has only $2,300 of equipment support, as opposed to $53,000 for the farm worker and $31,000 for the factory worker.

Office automation seeks to increase the efficiency with which organizational information flows are managed. Applications consist primarily of word processing, electronic mail, teleconferencing, and facsimile (scanned documents) transmission. The growth of office automation is linked to the continued technological development of the telecommunications industry, which provides the capability to link the individual stations and services within and between organizations.

Although electronic office automation equipment is relatively new, its growth, particularly for word processing, has been explosive. International Data Corporation (1980) estimates that word processing will grow at a rate of 50 percent at least until mid-decade, with 875,000 units installed by 1984 as compared to only 62,000 in 1979. Uttal (1982) estimates that word processing became a $4 billion industry in 1982.

The prognosis for electronic mail is less promising. The major problem is proliferation, rather than a standardization, of the technical options for networking. Companies are hesitant to make major investments in today's uncertain economic environment. The market potential for electronic mail was estimated to grow to between $200 and $650 million by 1982 (Yankee Group, 1979). The size of the market for electronic mail ultimately depends on whether the new telecommunication systems become fully operational and offer economic advantages over current mail delivery for communicating messages electronically. Some companies, such as Texas Instruments, have pioneered their own internal electronic mail systems. Craig (1981) and International Data Corporation (1980) provide descriptions of the operational characteristics of these systems.

An intermediary version of electronic mail has been proposed by the U.S. Postal Service. Under their proposal, messages would be sent electronically to a post office, where the physical document is created and then delivered by a letter carrier. The issue of who will control an intercompany electronic message service is currently one of the hottest regulatory issues in Washington. Indications are that the Postal Service will not be given a monopoly over electronic mail and that other carriers will be allowed to operate.

The goal of electronic mail, however, is not only to speed up the delivery of messages and facsimile documents, but also to expand the opportunities for teleconferencing. The major advantages of teleconferencing are potential savings in travel time and cost. Teleconferencing has not, however, been expanding rapidly—despite the rising costs of travel. International Data Corporation (1980) estimates the current market for teleconferencing to be only $70 to $80 million. While teleconferencing holds much promise, it has floundered in part because of technical limitations inherent in existing technology and in part because of the traditions of doing business face to face. Tyler (1981) and Johansen, Valee, and Spangler (1979) provide useful overviews of the advantages and limitations of various forms of teleconferencing for particular types of meetings and activities. Due to technical uncertainties and questions of social acceptability or benefits, it is not feasible at this time to project the growth of teleconferencing in the private sector.

The use of teleconferencing for public-sector agencies is even more problematic. Lucas (1981) notes that no single public agency has enough demand to support a service and there was no mechanism to aggregate demand and procure services. One approach that is being tried is the use of telecommunication brokers. The National Telecommunications and Information Agency (NTIA) has a charge to support several entrepreneurial organizations whose role will be to purchase telecommunication services from commercial carriers and then sell these services to public agencies on a retail basis. It is still too early to tell what effect this approach is going to have.

Overall, however, it is clear that office automation in one form or another is going to proceed at a rapid pace. One likely effect of this automation will be to make low-end white-collar workers vulnerable to job displacement (the extent is not clear). The major effect, however, will be changes in the way white-collar workers work. White-collar work will increasingly become information work that involves performing logical operations on electronicized information, for clerical workers as well as managers. Porat (1977) estimates that by 1985, one-fourth of the labor force, or 25 million workers, will be involved in transferring electronic data from one form to another. Giuliano (1982) estimates that by the end of the decade almost 40 percent of workers will be making daily use of electronic equipment. *These projections suggest that the computer will meet the criterion of a primary work tool by mid-decade.*

Strassman (1980) has done the most careful assessment of the implications of office automation for the nature of work and suggests the need to reorient traditional functional relationships in organizations in favor of an information middleman approach. The prototype of the information middleman is the clerk in the airline terminal who can instantaneously arrange for a wide variety of interrelated services (services that cut across many different functional areas of the airline and other companies) from a single station. Strassman sees this concept extended to many other service areas, such as financial management.

7. DATA BASES AND INFORMATION UTILITIES

While the previous section focused on using telecommunications to *manage the flow* of information and messages in business, an increasingly important function of telecommunications will be to *provide access* to information for both businesses and consumers. The issue of how to gain access to needed information has become critical; the amount of information produced has been increasing geometrically, whereas the amount of information individuals can absorb has remained relatively fixed. Under such conditions, the market for any particular piece of information declines, and the reading, or "accessing," of information becomes increasingly selective.

As an example of the effects of information expansion and its consequences, Lancaster (1978) notes that the number of science and technology periodicals doubled between 1965 and 1977. Despite this increase, the selectivity desired by readers grew faster than publishers could create specialized publications. As a result, an individual may still have to pay for twenty or thirty articles in a journal issue to get at the one article of direct interest. The purchase of extraneous material may be an acceptable strategy as long as the cost of the journal is low. The costs (and delays) of producing and distributing paper text, however, are rising so rapidly that a strategy of selective use of paper text is becoming less feasible. As a result, Lancaster (1978) concludes that present methods of physically distributing and storing text are inadequate to support the needs of scholars. This is true for businesspersons and scientists, as well as for consumers seeking information on a wide range of topics.

The limitations of paper text, combined with the growing availability of computers with low-cost digital storage and telecommunication capabilities, have led to the increased use of on-line (immediately accessible) electronic data bases. The electronic data base is as fundamental to the distribution of text as was Gutenberg's printing press. *Whereas the printing press made possible the distribution of large numbers of physical copies of text, the electronic data base makes it possible to distribute text without having to distribute multiple physical copies—a form of electronic paper.*

Business Week (August 17, 1981) quotes an IBM analyst as predicting that the total amount of characters stored electronically on-line would increase from the 1.7 trillion to 12 trillion by 1985. There is no reason to expect the trend to slow down after 1985, given the near certainty that storage, computing, and telecommunication costs will continue to decline as the need for information increases. This rapid growth of electronic forms of information is creating new types of services and computer applications. English-like data base retrieval languages are providing nontechnicians the capability to interact with corporate data bases. This will dramatically increase the number of individuals who routinely use the computer as work tools.

The number of services selling electronic information to businesses and consumers is also increasing, as are the technological options for accessing such data bases. *Business Week* (June 29, 1981) reports that 800 computerized information services are available, and the revenues from those systems are expected to grow from $600 million in 1981 to $3 billion in 1985. Data base services provide access to a wide range of information: business statistics, economic projections, merchandise sales, stock quotations, news services, airline schedules, and so on.

There are many technological options for delivering electronic information to customers. Information utilities such as Source and Compuserve provide access to data bases via telephone lines connected to computers. Videotex (two-way) and teletext (one-way) transmit data to the home or office via television signals carried by antenna, coaxial cable, or satellite. The signals are then separated by a special decoder that enables either the data or the television program to be displayed.

Cable systems have high-speed, two-way interactive capabilities that make it possible for homes with computers and/or storage devices to receive data at speeds up to several million bits per second. Such high speeds make it possible to scan or transmit large amounts of information. This creates the potential for applications such as electronic home study centers or electronic publishing. With such a capability, an individual in Tucson could scan text from a central library in Washington, D.C., or a publisher in New York, ordering the desired pages to be sent electronically to the home or local library. This capability has led Dunn (1980) to speculate that libraries will eventually become centers for making and distributing physical copies of electronic books, rather than loan sources. Other home applications made possible by cable include electronic mail, electronic shopping, and security monitoring.

While most of the on-line storage will be used for business applications, consumer use of electronic data bases will also increase during this decade. A number of companies are now planning to market the home terminals that will broaden the market of consumers who can tap into electronic data bases. AT&T and IBM are becoming active in videotex; the former is expected to market a $400 keypad terminal by 1984. According to the *Wall Street Journal* (June 12, 1981), Microcosmos has developed a $300 microterminal for home communication with large computers to do banking, pay bills, play games, and turn household appliances on and off. The cost could drop to $100 by 1982. More sophisticated home terminals are expected to be marketed by Novation; these terminals will enable home telephones and televisions to access data bases, at an expected cost of $300 by the end of 1982. Radio Shack now sells a $400 videotex terminal and a $30 software package that enables users to access a wide variety of electronic data bases, foreign news services, and electronic mail service. Several of the electronic game manufacturers are planning to sell attachments that will enable the machines to function as home terminals.

The ability of consumers to link these home terminals to coaxial cable systems, with their inherent advantages over telephone lines, is also increasing. Goldman (1980) notes that 15 million (or 20 percent) of the nation's households are now connected to cable services and that the figure is growing at about 15 percent annually. Nanus et al. (1981) project that the number of homes connected to cable will be 50 million by the mid-nineties. The same study notes that 98 percent of homes already have the equipment necessary for accessing information utilities (i.e., televisions and telephones).

It is also becoming increasingly feasible to use the home terminals to access data directly from satellite signals as it becomes possible to transmit satellite signals containing entertainment or data directly to the home (bypassing local television stations). For instance, the Federal Communications Commission (FCC) has given Communications Satellite Corporation (a subsidiary of COMSAT) the right to offer three new television channels that would be beamed from satellites to receiving dishes mounted on housetops. The dishes are projected to cost approximately $100 to $200 by 1985. As with so many of the home technologies, the initial incentive for acquiring satellite receptors will be new entertainment opportunities. The presence of these receptors will, however, begin to create new marketing opportunities that will stimulate the development of other services for home delivery via the receptor.

As low-cost equipment for accessing electronic data bases from the home becomes available, vendors will begin to increase the number of services they offer. Nanus et al. (1981) found thirty-six consumer network services already in existence. AT & T is attempting to experiment with electronic Yellow Pages but so far has encountered stiff opposition from newspaper publishers. Sears is planning to experiment with offering its catalog on video disks for individuals with video disk players. The video disk version would add motion pictures and sound to the existing text-and-picture method of displaying products. Radio Shack has joined with an Ohio newspaper to provide the first electronic newspaper. The French have announced plans to replace phone books with videotex. Urrows and Urrows (1981) report that the goal of the French plan is to put 30 million free terminals in homes by 1992 at a cost less than the $230 million currently spent to supply printed telephone books. The most comprehensive videotex system to date is Prestel in Britain, which offers 200,000 pages of on-line information, much of it free to users.

Trying to make projections about the rate of growth for information utilities and videotex is complicated by the relative newness of the service. While the evidence is clear that business is willing to pay for information, the record is less clear for typical consumers. For example, Lu (1981) notes that financial data bases such as the Dow Jones System and legal data bases (among others) can charge $60 to $150 per hour of connect time and still attract users. An upper limit on what consumers are likely to be willing to pay for data base access appears to be $15 per connect hour. In 1981, MicroNET and Source cost about $4 to $10 per hour but were not profitable because there were fewer than 10,000 users apiece. In both cases, most users are computer hobbyists, since the cost is substantially higher than acquiring the information from noncomputer sources.

The future course of videotex in this country is also unclear due to marketing and technological uncertainties. A number of experiments are currently being conducted in this country (which to date has lagged behind the Europeans in working with videotex) to determine the types of information in which consumers and other constituencies are interested. The experiments are also trying to determine how much they might be willing to pay for particular types of information and what the preferred modes of screen presentations are (see Dunn, 1980, and Elton & Carey, 1980, for a description of ongoing experiments). The development of a market in the United States is being delayed further by the fact that AT & T and IBM are developing different videotex standards.

The trends of reduced equipment and service costs, combined with the increasing cost of travel (for shopping) and paper text material, may eventually make accessing electronic data bases more attractive to consumers, particularly those who already have the necessary equipment. The Delphi panel from the Nilles et al. (1980) study did attempt to project future consumer uses. The results of this study, which are shown in Table 2, project an information utility market of $50 million by the end of this decade—a substantial growth rate but hardly a major industry. If the growth rate persists, however, it would result in a substantial industry in the next decade. Such an assumption is not unreasonable, given continued progress in reducing communication costs. Only about 7 to 8 percent of households are projected to be using system capabilities for electronic mail by the end of the decade.

TABLE 2   Projected Growth of Information Utility Services

	1978	1985	1990
Interactive network information service sales (millions of dollars)			
Small Business	1	6	16
Large Business	10	75	100
Education[a]	5	9	20
Home	—	10	50
No. of workers who use personal computers to reduce or eliminate the commute to work	—	0.5	1.0
No. of homes that can be reached via electronic mail	—	1.5	6.8
No. of homes using PCs for health monitoring	—	50K	300K

K = thousands
a. Includes Plato and similar systems
SOURCE: Nilles et al. (1980), pp. 3-22, 24.

It therefore appears that while microcomputers will become a cultural technology during this decade, they will be used primarily for entertainment and education. Sophisticated consumer use of applications such as electronic shopping will probably not be a major function until the next decade.

8. ARTIFICIAL INTELLIGENCE

The basic goal of artificial intelligence is to simulate human intelligence in machines. While there are various levels and degrees of intelligence, the primary objectives of artificial intelligence (AI) are to develop systems that can understand natural (human) languages and can learn to make judgments based on prior experience. While some argue that computers will never really be able to "think" and can only respond to direct instructions or preset strategies (and they may be right), major gains have been made in developing systems that appear to think. Such systems can perform tasks generally thought to require high levels of intelligence and creativity. The most common examples are the chess-playing programs, which can beat all but the top masters. A less publicized example is the Internist I, developed at the University of Pittsburgh, which was designed to diagnose the full range of adult illnesses. In a recent test, the computer system did not perform as well as the internists on duty, but the performances were close. It appears that Caduceus (another medical AI program under development; see Waldholz, 1982) will be better.

Another example of AI is Eurisko, a program developed at Xerox's Palo Alto Research Center, which can discover and apply heuristics. This program recently designed a strategy to beat all human opponents at Traveller, a highly complex futuristic war game (Alexander, 1982a).

There have also been advances in the ability of computers to interpret instructions written in natural languages. Such a capability could greatly simplify the process of communicating with a computer. Several companies have developed systems that can accept instructions written in English as input. By and large, these programs are available only on very large and expensive computers. A program released in 1982, called SAVVY, enables the user to teach a computer a language that thereafter becomes the language of interaction. What is particularly amazing about this program is that it runs on a microcomputer.

There are many potential industrial, military, and educational uses for AI. Widespread use requires the development of better algorithms to simulate thinking and greater understanding of the processes involved in general learning and the learning of specific skills. Low-cost, highly powerful computers are also needed.

Given the promising rate at which AI algorithms have developed over the past decade and the high probability that there will be dramatic increases in available computer power per unit cost in this decade, there is no longer any question that AI is feasible. The only question is when, and for what types of applications. For example, AI researchers have found that it is easier to develop systems that mimic the expert intelligence of doctors and chemists than the process in which a four-year-old child engages when learning the fundamentals of logic (Alexander, 1982). While it is easy to predict the development of the hardware, the evolution of the algorithms themselves is less clear. As a result, while interest and investment in AI are increasing and limited applications are being implemented, widespread use of AI capabilities will probably not occur until around the end of this decade. AI will, however, make possible the implementation of intelligent robots (which can "see" and "feel") by mid-decade.

9. INCENTIVES TO INNOVATE

Since the availability of new technology is in itself no incentive for its adoption, incredibly powerful economic and possibly social forces are necessary for a society to adopt these new technologies and incur the type of dislocative effects that have been described. What forces are promoting the use of computer-based technology? Are they powerful enough to sustain the adoption process over the coming decade, or will all this new technology merely become an electronic Edsel?

The two basic forces promoting adoption of the new technologies are (a) the need to be competitive in a worldwide economy and (b) the general desire to increase living standards. The lowering of trade barriers and the availability of credit have dramatically increased the amount of international trade, to the point that one can talk about a global economy. At the same time, the technological and industrial supremacy that the United States enjoyed at the end of World War II has eroded. The Europeans have learned how to pool their R&D resources and have become competitive in sophisticated technologies such as aeronautical engineering, biogenetics, and alternative energy (particularly nuclear energy). The Japanese have also developed tremendous marketing and organizational skills.

Our overseas competitors have likewise become more proficient in using their new technology to improve productivity. The aggressive Japanese robotics program has enabled Japan's automobile workers to be far more productive than their American counterparts. Even using the more restrictive American definition of what a robot actually is, Masayoshi (1981) found that the Japanese have installed, and are producing, almost three times as many robots as the United States. The failure to take aggressive advantage of the capabilities of robots is symptomatic of the tendency of American business in the previous decade to invest in labor rather than in other forms of capital, such as plants and equipment (Gallese, 1980). As American business became increasingly undercapitalized, productivity stagnated, remaining essentially unchanged in the 1977-81 period (*Monthly Labor Review,* 1982). According to the World Bank, the United States slipped to ninth place among the industrialized nations in output per person in 1980. (While U.S. productivity has risen in 1983, it remains to be seen whether that is merely reflective of massive layoffs or whether business will begin to make the needed capital investments.)

The productivity advantage of some of our international competitors has had a devastating impact on our domestic auto and electronics industries. If U.S. automobile companies are to regain lost market shares, they must follow the Japanese lead; and as everyone knows, what is good for General Motors is good for the USA. All manufacturing industries that want to remain competitive in a global economy are going to have to automate production as much as possible. The productivity battle is now being joined in the semiconductor industry, which produces the building blocks of the new technologies. The stakes are enormous. The electronics industry currently does $100 billion in annual sales, which may grow to $400 billion by the end of the decade (Norman, 1981). The electronics industry is even more critical than its own sales figures indicate, since almost every manufactured product in the world will depend to some degree on advanced electronic components. Whoever dominates the semiconductor industry controls the world economy in the 1990s.

The issue of productivity enhancement is also critical to the second societal force promoting the use of the new technologies: the drive for higher standards of living. Under conditions of declining productivity, average real income, as opposed to inflated income, declines. The highly undercapitalized state of American industry in 1980, combined with the increases in labor and energy costs (particularly for plants with inefficient equipment) that occurred during the seventies, has rendered it virtually impossible to continue to increase productivity (or real income) using the former strategy of increasing labor intensity. Those who want their standard of living raised and are not threatened with job displacement will be potent political supporters of reindustrializing with, and making large investments in, the new technologies.

In addition to political pressure, the technologies create their own incentive for utilization. The efficiency advantages of the new technologies are simply too overwhelming to ignore and are sufficiently large to stimulate organizations to expend the energy and resources needed to implement them, regardless of potential risks. Modern robots cost $4.80 an hour and often replace one to five workers, each earning $15 to $20 per hour. Computer-aided design (CAD) can reduce the time needed to develop and test prototypes from months and years to days. It is more difficult to document and realize direct benefits from office automation technology. Giuliano (1982) estimates that the transition to word processing from multidraft typing can reduce secretarial costs from more than $7 per letter to less than $2; electronic mail would bring the cost down to $.30. A quasi-experimental study by Tapscott (1982) found that the introduction of basic office automation capabilities resulted in a 10 percent time savings. In addition, new techniques are being developed at training institutions to help managers realize the benefits of these technologies (Tyler, 1981).

Individuals may find other types of benefits sufficiently attractive to push for the use of these technologies. One is the potential to affect lifestyles by changing the way we work. For example, Cole (1981) cites results showing that dispersing the workplace by substituting telecommunication access for at least part of the daily commute to central urban locations can produce a benefit-cost ratio of 4:1, even before reduced transportation costs are taken into account. Others suggest the possibility that telecommunications may almost eliminate the need to commute ("telecommute") for large numbers of workers (see Heltz & Turoff, 1978, and Toffler, 1980, for discussions of the social implications of telecommuting). It is not likely, however, that individuals will want to eliminate working in central locations because, as the Naisbitt Group (1981) points out, individuals in high-tech environments also seek "high-touch" environments (i.e., those with high levels of human interaction). The benefits of limited commuting to decentralized work centers would be enormous in terms of the environment, energy consumption, and the human psyche.

The benefits of the new technology apply not only to large corporations but also to small businesses. Tyler (1981) notes that telecommunications provides, for the first time, the capability for individuals, or
small businesses with single offices, to serve national or international
markets with their "information products." In addition, not all the benefits go to business. Dunn and Ray (1979) estimate potential benefits
to consumers on the order of $50 to $150 billion per year from having
access to "better" information in electronic data bases.

As a result, it appears that the economic incentives to adopt the new
technologies are sufficiently powerful to maintain, and in some cases
accelerate, existing trends throughout this decade. In addition, the diffuse nature of the benefits is such that there will probably be strong
(but far from unanimous) political support for their use. Indeed, the
trend toward increasing use of high technology is already beginning to
change the nature of the business environment.

10. IMPLICATIONS FOR THE
BUSINESS AND REGULATORY ENVIRONMENT

There are two indications of the profound changes that the new
technologies are causing in the business environment. The first is the
amount of corporate investment for acquisitions and R & D. The second indicator of the significance of the technological changes is the
extent to which they are requiring an almost total revision of existing
regulatory policies and creating whole new legal traditions.

With respect to the investment indicator, there are no exact data on
the total investment being made by major corporations to develop
new technology. Such investments by a handful of companies in telecommunications alone will almost certainly be in the billions of dollars before 1985. In addition, these investments represent not only
money but also a major realignment of the competitive territoriality
of the largest corporation in this society, territorialities that have persisted for at least two decades. It is a corporate environment in which
AT & T is taking aim at competing with IBM, Xerox with AT & T,
IBM with AT & T and newspaper publishers, COMSAT with CBS,
Sears Roebuck with Bank of America, and Exxon with everyone.

There are several reasons for this realignment. The first is opportunity. As businesses become more dependent on computers and telecommunications, they can enter more fields, because a computer can be programmed to perform multiple functions. There are many areas of the service industry where the ability to provide a particular service is a function of having capital and appropriate software (and possibly regulatory permission). This is happening to a large extent in the financial services industries as insurance companies become stockbrokers, stockbrokerage houses compete with banks, department stores compete with banks, and banks compete with money market funds.

Another cause of the competitive realignment is that new business opportunities are opening up as the economy undergoes fundamental change—opportunities that are likely to be the major growth industries over the next two decades. In addition to the profit potentials from entering these businesses, major corporations fear that failure to do so will restrict their future growth opportunities. IBM, in recognition of the enormous stakes that exist in telecommunications, has overcome its traditional resistance to being a regulated business and is now subjecting itself to FCC oversight. AT&T, on the other hand, the largest regulated business in the world, has reversed government policy and will be allowed to set up unregulated subsidiaries that will compete in the computer field. Both companies are also planning to enter the new fields of videotex and a variety of other networked services. IBM is also entering the robotics field.

The second indication of the profound nature of the changes in the business environment is the inability of existing regulatory provisions to deal with a whole host of new issues being raised by new technological capabilities. Tydeman and Lipinski (1980) provide an overview of new regulatory issues raised by the use of videotex, while Yurow (1981) discusses telecommunications regulatory policy. Tracing the regulatory implications of changing technology is well beyond the scope of this book (which is unfortunate, since they are quite intriguing). The following passage from Tydeman and Lipinski (1980), discussing the regulatory implications of videotex, is, however, illustrative:

> Videotex brings together a highly regulated industry (communication) and a relatively unregulated industry (data processing and computing).

Under the current law, the FCC has principal regulatory jurisdiction over broadcast teletext. This body is currently wrestling with the regulatory dividing line between data processing and communication, a line that videotex straddles. But videotex may also be involved in some way with other governmental bodies, such as the Federal Trade Commission, the Justice Department, the Copyright Tribunal, the National Telecommunications and Information Administration, the courts, state public utility commissions, and the Comptroller of Currency. The uncertainty here begins with uncertainty about who regulates whom, but even more important are questions about the nature of the regulation. Who monitors the various regulations? How are they implemented? What are the implications of such regulations for suppliers of the service, information providers, information content, and users of videotex? In particular, what areas of regulation are likely to be in conflict or to impinge upon each other? (pp. 6, 7)

The resolution of these types of regulatory questions has fundamental implications for reshaping the political arrangements within and between levels of government. The new technology also raises questions about the basic organizational structure of government. In the federal government, for example, the Federal Communications Commission (FCC) sets communication policy, the National Bureau of Standards (NBS) and the General Accounting Office (GAO) set computer procurement policy, the Office of Management and Budget (OMB) manages data acquisition, and the National Telecommunications and Information Administration (NTIA) is in charge of telecommunication policy. Technology has, however, rendered these functional categories indistinct.

11. A SCENARIO OF TECHNOLOGY EVENTS

Previous sections have reviewed assessments of the environmental impacts of technology during this decade. This section will consolidate that information into technology events that describe the nature and extent to which computers will become a cultural and primary work tool during this decade.

The basic pattern that emerges from the technology assessments that have been reviewed is that sophisticated business use of new technology seems to be half a decade ahead of consumer use. Business is now making heavy and rapidly increasing use of basic applications in data processing, office automation, and robotics. Business use of more sophisticated applications such as distributed data processing, electronic mail, or teleconferencing will probably not occur on a large scale till the second half of this decade. Large-scale use of highly sophisticated applications such as the automated assembly line, direct voice input, and telecommuting will probably have to wait for the first half of the next decade.

The primary process of implementation will be a phasing in, rather than immediate large-scale use of, sophisticated applications, because of the need to change traditional practices if the potential benefits of technology are to be realized. A phasing in approach will also result from the need for additional technological developments in telecommunications, computers, and artificial intelligence.

The scenario for technology in the home is less clear. Large numbers of computers will appear in perhaps as many as half the nation's households by the end of this decade. These will be used largely as stand-along units purchased mostly (initially) for entertainment purposes and interconnected with the television. Low-cost interconnection capability to telephones, hi-fi systems, and cable and satellite receptors will become available and may start to be used by mid-decade, again largely to integrate home entertainment opportunities. More sophisticated home applications such as home shopping, bill paying, and energy management will begin during mid-decade but probably will not be used on a very large scale till the next decade.

The extent to which home-based technology will be used for educational purposes or for linking with electronic data bases remains to be seen, although such use will increase in the latter half of the decade. Also unknown are the mechanisms by which such substitutions will begin to occur. Will the transition of computer use from entertainment and convenience tool to an educational device result largely from the desire of computer-literate parents to transmit these skills to their children? Will it result spontaneously from children's natural curiosity about devices that provide pleasure? Will it result from parent dissatisfaction with the public school system? Can, and should, government play a role in facilitating such a transition? In any event, it does appear that there will be extensive amounts of home educational software available by 1984-85, perhaps earlier.

Given the existence of a phasing-in process (in both home and workplace), technology events will be described in terms of the points in time when widespread shifts to more sophisticated forms of use can be expected to occur based on the fairly consistent patterns that emerge from the literature review. Table 3 summarizes the projected technology events for this decade and the next.

The basic purpose of this assessment has been to try to estimate the point in time by which the computer will become both a cultural technology (defined as being in 10 percent of homes) and a primary work tool (involving 25 percent of jobs). According to the literature reviewed in sections 3 and 6 of this chapter, that technology event will begin around mid-decade and will intensify from that point on.

If 1985-87 is the point in time when computers and their progeny will meet the dual criterion of being a cultural technology and a primary work tool, that is also the period (under the basic hypothesis of this chapter) when major educational needs for training individuals to use the technology will exist in the environment and when significant external demands to provide such training will have an impact on the schools. This provides a cushion of three to four years for schools and governmental policy to prepare for the needed adjustments.

Before one can begin to discuss the issue of what kinds of policies are needed to help schools prepare for the anticipated new set of needs and demands, the following questions must first be answered:

(a) What kinds of new educational programs will be needed?
(b) To what extent are schools now providing such programs?

These questions will be discussed in the next chapter.

TABLE 3 Environmental Technology Events

	1980-85	1985-87	1987-90	1990-
Home uses of technology	Increasing use for entertainment and simple applications.	Found in 10% of homes—shift to educational uses begins.	Found in about 40% of homes, increasingly used for accessing electronic data bases and home education.	Extensive use accessing electronic data bases and home education. Found in the majority of homes.
Workplace uses of technology	Extensive use for technicians and clerks. Minor implications for blue-collar work.	Use required in 25% of jobs, increasing use of robots and electronic mail.	Growing use by nontechnician managers, increasing replacement of blue-collar work by intelligent robots, growing dependence on sophisticated office automation applications such as electronic mail.	Basic tool used for managing communications and conferences. Large-scale replacement of blue-collar work and other routine work. Direct voice input.

II
THE NEW TECHNOLOGY
AND EDUCATIONAL NEEDS

THROUGHOUT THE HISTORY of our nation, whenever new technologies became cultural technologies and/or primary work tools, schools have had to expand their curricula. The production line generated vocational education, the car necessitated driver education, and the printing press created the need for schools to teach reading. It can therefore be expected that as the computer becomes both a cultural technology and a primary work tool during the 1985-87 period, it will generate the need for new educational services. The changes in the home, workplace, and society in general will cause a shift or expansion in the kinds of educational services that are needed and demanded. And this point in time, it appears that the new technology will generate the following curriculum needs:

(a) the need for workers to have the skills necessary for jobs in the changed labor market, as well as the need to have a labor force with adequate technical skills;

(b) the need for consumers and parents to obtain needed, or useful, services from the new technology; and

(c) the need for voters to make informed choices about the myriad social and political issues related to technology that will have to be resolved in the coming decade and a half.

The following sections will discuss each of these needs as well as their curricular implications.

1. THE CHANGING LABOR FORCE

As suggested in the previous chapter, in this decade substantial inroads will be made in automating routine work processes. Blue- and white-collar work is going to shift away from literal or repetitive tasks toward more flexible and logical interactions with electronic forms of information and information workers. Simple office and factory work is going to be replaced, much as the farm laborer was replaced by the tractor.

The issue of whether this new automation will merely alter the nature of work or will substantially reduce the number of jobs is not clear. The American economy has survived many automation shocks over the centuries. It takes only 3 percent of the labor force to feed the population (and produce a large surplus) and only 1 percent to provide the vast majority of the mineral needs of this nation. It takes only a few dozen switchboard operators to handle a million long-distance calls, a task that would have required several thousand workers thirty years ago (Leontief, 1982). To date, however, these automation shocks have not reduced the total number of jobs.

After reviewing the optimistic and doomsday predictions of how the new technologies will affect employment, Nilles et al. (1980) concluded that there was not yet any basis for determining impact on the total number of jobs. The Bureau of Labor Statistics expects the work force to grow about 25 percent during this decade (Main, 1982b). Leontief (1982), on the other hand, has produced analyses suggesting that the new technology will increase unemployment unless the trend toward reducing the workweek is resumed after a thirty-five year period during which the forty-hour workweek remained the norm. Whether such a gloomy prognosis proves true remains to be seen, but even if it does there is a clear policy option for coping with it.

There are much better data on shifts occurring in the labor force. Economist Marc Porat (1977) has done the most careful and comprehensive (albeit controversial) analysis of the information sector of the U.S. economy. Porat concludes that the information sector grew from 15 percent of the work force in 1910 to over 40 percent by 1970. Even more significant, Porat found that information workers earned over 53 percent of all labor income in 1967. This means that we no longer have an industrial economy; it is now an information economy. Just as agricultural workers, as a percentage of the total labor work force, continued to decline once we entered the industrial phase, the percentage of the labor force employed in manufacturing will continue to decline now that we have become an information (postindustrial?) economy. Ginzberg (1982) notes that 90 percent of all new jobs added to the economy from 1969 to 1976 were in services rather than manufacturing. Porat estimates that 50 million information workers (approximately 50 percent of the projected labor force) will be needed by 1985.

There is a good bit of circumstantial evidence to support the existence of a trend toward information work. Nilles et al. (1980) did a spot-check of 5,000 advertised job openings in the classified section of the *Los Angeles Times* and found that 75 percent were for knowledge workers. This same study cites a finding by Arthur Luehrman, of the Lawrence Hall of Science, that 80 percent of new jobs in Pacific Gas and Electric Company require computer understanding. As early as 1971, 57 percent of the jobs in the then fledgling semiconductor industry could be classified as information work, with only 36 percent employed in semiskilled jobs.

Changes in skill requirements are also occurring in the traditional manufacturing industries. Lund (1981) found that when metalworking jobs were replaced by simpler light electronic assembly (as electronics replaced mechanical parts in products), production and service jobs tend to be deskilled but the work of engineers and supervisors becomes more demanding. Hymowitz (1981) reports that General Motors, which now employs one skilled worker for every 5.6 assembly line workers, may need a one-to-one ratio by the year 2000. Although jobs involved in mechanical repair are also expected to grow, they will increasingly require a knowledge of electronics. At the same time, many white-collar skill positions in manufacturing, such as drafting, will be displaced by computer-aided design technology.

Levin and Rumberger (1983) argue that rather than increasing the demand for skilled workers, technology will have the opposite effect. They argue that so many jobs will be deskilled as a result of technology, the demand for technical workers will not increase substantially.

Their conclusions are based on Bureau of Labor Statistics (BLS) projections and analysis of past experiences with automation in industrial production. Such projections must, however, be viewed at the present time as highly suspect, given that the economy is changing so rapidly and the nature of the transition is so unique. In addition, the position of Levin and Rumberger is contrary to the present experience of escalating demand for technical skills in the early stages of the transition. At the same time, such increases will not continue indefinitely, and it is not likely that the *majority* of jobs will ever require *extremely high* levels of technical skills.

It is likely that there will be a major increase in service-sector jobs that interface between the public and the technology. Many of them will be deskilled jobs that depend on personality. For example, the BLS expects that the fastest-growing occupation in this decade will be the fast-food worker. Other service workers, however, will have to interface with much more sophisticated technology, which will require high levels of skill.

While there will clearly be employment opportunities for deskilled or low-skilled jobs in the eighties, the competition for such jobs will be enormous. Education will therefore be even more of a prerequisite for employment opportunities in emerging semi- and high technical skill jobs. A significant portion of the work force is going to have to acquire new work skills and habits in the near future. Many of these new skills will relate to using technology, and a large percentage of the growing nonmanufacturing workers are going to have to begin to perform increasingly sophisticated technical and analytic work.

Consider, as an example of increasing sophistication, the case of clerical work. It is fairly easy now for secretaries to adapt to office automation since, in its present form, it only substitutes one form of typing machine for another. The grammatical and vocabulary skills of the clerks are still the primary determinant of office productivity. There are, however, systems currently on the market that check text for spelling errors and make automatic corrections. The next generation of word processors (around 1984) will automatically check spelling and some aspects of grammar. At that point, clerical work will be somewhat deskilled. As a consequence, moreover, increasing numbers of information workers will find it advantageous to use the capabilities of the word processors to compose and edit the original versions of their work by themselves. In one experiment, Tapscott (1982) found that the professional staff in an office automation environment tended to compose and edit up to 75 percent of their text-generation activities on their own.

When clerical work becomes highly automated, the clerical work force will have to take on additional, or different, functions in order to justify its existence. This will be particularly true when, around 1990, direct voice input, which will eliminate almost all manual work involved in producing text, becomes available. The substitute clerical tasks will probably involve forms of nonroutine interactions with data bases that require performing linear-logic technical operations. The duties of the clerical worker are thus displaced and are replaced with higher-skilled work resembling that currently done by low-level programmers.

While traditionally routine work becomes more technical, there will also be a growing demand for those who are commonly viewed as technical workers: engineers and programmers. Anders (1981) noted that although there was a demand for 54,000 additional programmers, the nation's colleges graduated only 11,000 people with bachelor's degrees in the field in 1980. At a time of high youth unemployment, high school students with a good background in programming may be able to earn as much as a beginning college professor. Anders reports that the demand for programmers may double during this decade, and *Business Week* (September 1, 1980) estimates that it may triple to 1.5 million by 1990. Major advances in programming productivity aids and/or artificial intelligence could suppress the growth somewhat in absolute terms, but the demand for programmers, particularly highly skilled ones, will remain strong and exceed supply for the foreseeable future. There will also be an increasing demand for individuals who can service and maintain the new technology.

Although, as already noted, it is impossible to predict at this point the impact of the new technology on the total number of jobs available, it is clear that there will be major changes in the distribution of jobs as well as shifts in the skill requirements of more traditional jobs. This trend is already becoming evident in the mature manufacturing industries. Estimates are that even after the economy recovers, as many as 200,000 of the unemployed automobile workers will never be reemployed in their previous occupations.

The major curricular implications of the employment trends inherent in the information economy, with its increasingly technical demands, are as follows:

(a) Increase the distribution of higher-order skills among students. This requires raising expectations for the majority of students and substituting discovery activities designed to stimulate logical thought for many of the rote activities in large portions of the curriculum.
(b) Strengthen the mathematics and science curriculum, particularly at the elementary levels.
(c) Provide all students several opportunities to use computers to produce a major project.
(d) Strengthen the curriculum in the areas of computer programming and electronics.
(e) Provide extensive retraining opportunities for adults, particularly those with good work records who have become victims of the new technology.

2. CONSUMER NEEDS

Consumer use of the new technology will take three main forms:

(a) taking advantage of entertainment and educational opportunities;
(b) electronic shopping; and
(c) engaging in self-service activities.

With respect to the latter, Ernst (1981) notes that the key to improving productivity in the growing service sector is to induce consumers to engage in self-service activities in return for convenience. An individual using an "automated bank teller" is really performing the operations that would otherwise be performed by a teller; in a sense the consumer is being conned by the term. The consumer is really undertaking a greater responsibility in the transaction than previously, in return for the conveniences of quicker service and around-the-clock banking. Of course, the greater the gain in convenience desired by the consumer, the more complicated the system must become, both for the system designer and the consumer-user. The technical sophistication of consumers could thus become a limiting factor in improving productivity in service sectors, or in limiting the benefits they can obtain from technology.

There is already some indication that consumers' lack of familiarity with branching (as opposed to sequential) searching techniques is creating problems in using electronic data bases. For most individuals, accessing information currently consists of using the dictionary and reading a newspaper. Looking for information in a dictionary or newspaper, however, is essentially a two-step sequential process in which (in the former case) you search for a letter and then search within the section devoted to that letter. Using the searching capability of the computer may require the user to specify ten different conditions in response to a series of menus appearing in sequence, each new menu usually selected on the basis of responses to previous ones. Lu (1981) notes that most people are unwilling to go through more than two steps to find a piece of information. A study of Holland's interactive videotex system revealed that users initiated search procedures correctly in only 56 percent of the attempts; 30 percent of the searches failed completely.

The major curricular implication of this section is the need to provide the opportunity for students to engage in data base searching activities on a computer. Such activities could be provided by a computer-based library cataloging system or by giving students access to computer network services such as GIS (Guidance Information System) or an information utility such as Source. Prince (1981) describes the impact of the latter type of program.

3. VOTER LITERACY

Voters are going to be asked to express preferences on a wide variety of issues related to the role and use of technology in society. These issues range from supporting school curricula related to the use of technology to economic protectionism versus reindustrialization. Some will view protectionism as a solution to the problem of disappearing jobs. A policy that relies primarily or solely on protectionism, however, is more likely to shrink the overall international market, drastically reducing overseas markets for American goods and creating massive defaults by foreign countries on monies owed to U.S. banks.

The real solution to the problems raised by technological change, if there is one, has to be based on a series of enlightened, nontraditional governmental policies and management strategies. Such policies require shifting government subsidies and incentives from traditional to emerging industries. The solution will also require American management to be more aggressive and take a longer-term view of investment payoffs, particularly those related to R & D. Getting American industry back in shape also requires the use of techniques to reduce the adversarial relationship between management and labor, and both must pay greater attention to the details of producing higher-quality goods. Ouchi (1981) and Hayes and Abernathy (1980) have done the most work in developing specific proposals for revitalizing American management practices.

There is some evidence that the Japanese are not invincible and that aggressive American business practices can meet their challenge, particularly in the high-tech area. For example, the Japanese penetration of the American 64K-bit chip market reached 75 percent in 1980 but was beaten back to under 50 percent in 1982 by the adoption of superior production technology by U.S. companies. In addition, the Japanese have been relatively unsuccessful in penetrating the American microcomputer, international software, and mainframe markets. The Japanese are, however, spending massive amounts of R & D monies to beat the U.S. in producing the fifth-generation mainframe computer—one that will combine elements of artificial intelligence. Enlightened government and industry policy must keep this from happening.

If a Luddite reaction to the consequences of the new technologies is to be avoided, and if taxpayers, government officials, and managers are to adopt needed new perspectives and funding programs under conditions of adversity, it is important these individuals have at least some familiarity with the technologies. It is also important that they know the potential benefits, as well as potential problems, from the use of these technologies, which will help them weigh the pros and cons of various technology-related policy initiatives at all levels of government.

The curricular implications of voter needs are for computer literacy programs that provide not only some basic knowledge about the computer and technology but also students with access to professionals in the field. Such programs should offer opportunities to explore the implications of using the new technologies, and to integrate such activities into general citizenship, civics, and social studies activities and programs.

4. ADEQUACY OF THE EXISTING SCHOOL CURRICULUM

With respect to the educational needs discussed in the previous sections, the most critical need at the elementary-secondary level over the short term is for technical training. How adequate is the existing curriculum in that regard? Izaak Wurszup, at the University of Chicago, has been arguing persuasively that the math programs in Russia are far superior to our own and that this "math gap" constitutes a national security issue for the United States, since the Russians could achieve technological superiority. In response to such assertions, a joint National Science Foundation-Department of Education (NSF-DOE) presidential task force was convened in 1979 by President Carter to examine whether existing math and science programs were capable of supporting the technological development of this country.

The task force concluded that our system is producing adequate numbers of scientists to meet projected needs in most areas. Some worrisome shortages are expected in computer science and engineering. Of greater concern to the task force, however, was the deteriorating quality of math and science programs in the secondary schools, combined with declining standards and requirements for non-science majors. The report noted:

The general quality of science and mathematics instruction at the secondary level has deteriorated since the 1960's, as has the scientific and

> mathematical competence of students who are not motivated towards careers in science and engineering. (p. 7)

> There is today a growing discrepancy between the science, mathematics and technology education acquired by high school graduates who plan to follow scientific and engineering careers and those who do not. Scientific and technical literacy is increasingly necessary in our society, but the number of our young people who graduate from high school and college with only the most rudimentary notions of science, mathematics and technology portends trouble in the decades ahead. (p. VII)

The task force noted that a number of countries had reformed their curricula in the belief that increasing the degree of technical emphasis would increase their international economic competitiveness in a technological age. Japan, Germany, and the USSR have much more stringent math and science requirements for nonscientists and make greater use of those trained as scientists in public- and private-sector managerial positions. For example, *all* college-bound secondary students in Japan take four mathematics and three natural science courses. One consequence of these differences is that American youth rank fifteenth in the international science test (Tucker, 1982b). Lack of emphasis on science is also reflected in the fact that only 6 percent of U.S. students get higher-education degrees in science, as opposed to 21 percent in Japan (Tucker, 1982b). Peter Drucker notes:

> Since 1970, the number of engineers trained each year in Japan has tripled, while the U.S. has tripled the number of law school graduates and actually cut the number of engineering students. Japan now graduates each year as many engineers as all of Western Europe, and at least as many as the U.S., and most of those being recent graduates are just beginning to produce. (p. 26)

After noting that Britain's declining ability to compete in international trade was probably due to the decline in its engineering training, the task force attempted to assess the extent to which declining emphasis on science and math in the United States could jeopardize its future. The task force concluded:

Comparisons between the U.S. and our international competitors suggest that our eminence in basic research is secure. However, our ability to apply technology to our military and industrial pursuits may well be hampered by the relatively low level of scientific and mathematical competence of our non-scientists and, in some respects, by the apparent cooling of science interest among our students generally.

There is anecdotal evidence from U.S. industry that in some highly technical areas the time required to produce a product has increased as workers' base level of understanding of science and mathematics has decreased over the past decade. (p. 137)

The consequences of a sharp dichotomy between the training of scientists and nonscientists extends to the managerial level. In the United States, the scientist is viewed as a researcher and the manager as a lay person. The Japanese, on the other hand, overproduce scientists for research needs and place the excess in managerial positions. The task force noted that 50 percent of Japanese managers in the public and private sectors have science backgrounds, whereas the United States relies on individuals with legal and finance backgrounds. This greater familiarity with technology at the managerial level is related to the greater willingness of Japanese companies to adopt new technology at the expense of short-term profits and the tendency of the Japanese government to subsidize efforts to develop new technology.

Finally, although the task force concluded that the technical training of U.S. scientists appears to be adequate for future research and development needs, it pointed out notable exceptions in engineering and computer science. The latter shortage is beginning to constrict the growth of the computer industry. *Business Week* (September 1, 1981) estimates that the shortage of programmers could restrict the growth of the data processing industry by a third, or $30 billion, in 1983.

Although it is not certain that inadequate technical preparation of nonscientists will erode our international competitiveness, there is reason for concern even if the premise is only partially correct. There will be a temptation, when proposing solutions to this potential problem, to draw analogies to the Sputnik era. There are, however, fundamental differences between the circumstances and needs that prevailed in the late sixties and now. These differences are summarized in Table 4.

The basic differences are that the educational goals of the Sputnik era—e.g., to train more scientists— were fairly discrete, and they were enacted during a period of expansion. The current need to strengthen the technical knowledge of the non-science major is more diffuse and occurs during a period of contraction. As a result, a simple add-on approach, whereby math courses are added to existing programs, gifted students are given computers to work with, or extra textbooks are provided, does not address the current need. A more comprehensive curricular reform is needed in which the *average* student is exposed to more science, math, and computer use. This curricular objective requires a far more comprehensive reform than what occurred in the Sputnik era. (It must be emphasized, however, that while it is important to increase the math and science literacy of the average student, it is not necessary to try to train everyone to be a scientist.)

Achieving such comprehensive reform is particularly difficult at the critical elementary levels, where student attitudes are formed. The difficulties arise largely because of the lack of technical training and skills among teachers. Papert (1980) notes that most math instruction at the elementary level is devoted to learning arithmetic by rote as opposed to learning about relationships between quantities and events, such as motion, that are intrinsically interesting to children. In addi-

TABLE 4   Comparisons of Curricular Reform in the Post-Sputnik
and Post-1985 Eras

	Post-Sputnik Era	*Post-1985 Era*
Focus of educational need	Train Scientists	Prepare nonscientists for a technological age
Rationale for government intervention	National Defense	Maintain competitiveness in the global economy
Perceived competitors	Russia	Russia, Japan, France, Germany
Status of educational system	Expansion	Contraction

tion, math is taught largely by individuals who are terrified by the subject and in ways that appeal only to students with obsessive-compulsive personalities. It is a case of the frustrated teaching the impressionable via the same techniques that produced their own frustrations.

Perhaps even more disturbing than the inadequate training in technical areas is the apparent lack of emphasis on developing the general higher-order thinking skills of the vast majority of students. According to data collected by the National Assessment of Educational Progress (Forbes, 1982), the percentage of high school seniors who are able to demonstrate competence on a wide variety of higher-order thinking tasks has declined over the past decade. For example, the number of students who were able to complete a persuasive-writing task declined from 21 to 15 percent, and math problem solving declined from 33 to 29 percent (Forbes, 1982). As of 1980, the number of seniors who were unable to demonstrate basic competence in higher-order skills ranged from 38 to 85 percent, depending on the task. This study estimated that if present trends continue, by 1990 one to two million seniors will not have the essential skills to compete in the information economy.

There are also problems in higher education. Japan produces as many engineers as does the United States—with half the population. At the same time, because of faculty shortages, it is difficult for higher education in this country to increase the number of engineers and programmers substantially. Faculty in these areas are increasingly wooed into industry by high salaries and the opportunity to work with better equipment. Over 10 percent of available faculty positions go unfilled. In addition, the rewards are such that students are leaving graduate school earlier. Between 1969 and 1978 the annual output of engineering Ph.D.s declined by almost one-third, and math Ph.D.s by one-half (Simon & Grant, 1972; Grant & Eiden, 1981).

There is also the educational problem of retraining workers displaced by technology. Whether or not policies will emerge in this area remains to be seen. At this point, however, neither government, industry, labor unions nor educational institutions have figured out a strategy for dealing with what may become a major social problem.

In short, the existing educational system has major inadequacies, at all levels, in meeting the needs of a changing economy.

5. SUMMARY

There appear to be two unmet educational needs resulting from changing technology: (a) to train more computer programmers and engineers, and (b) to increase the technological sophistication and higher-order skills of nonscientists. While it cannot be proven conclusively that these needs are directly related to the national interests of military preparedness and economic expansion, there is anecdotal evidence that they are. This implies a role for federal and state policy.

There is, however, a fundamental difference between the two needs in terms of policy requirements. The first need is discrete and requires the expansion of existing programs for a particular category of student. The second educational need implies a far more comprehensive type of curricular reform that requires the creation of new services, and the modification of existing services, for *most* students. If it is indeed necessary to introduce such curricular change, the obvious questions are (a) Can it be done under the present conditions of contraction? and (b) What is the best way to attempt it? These questions are addressed in later chapters.

ALTERNATIVE APPROACHES TO DELIVERING SERVICES

IT WAS SUGGESTED in the previous chapter that changing technology is generating new educational needs that require comprehensive curricular reform. It was also suggested that such reform is in the national interest. Addressing such needs is, however, complicated by the contracting nature of education and failed reform attempts during the sixties and seventies. With respect to the latter, federal policy was successful in stimulating districts to adopt a variety of add-on programs. It was not, however, successful in stimulating reform of the "general" program for the "regular" students, and this general reform will be needed if schools are to adapt to the educational demands imposed by changing technology. The traditional approaches to curricular reform attempted during the sixties and seventies are unlikely, by themselves, to deliver the educational services needed in a highly technological age. Nontraditional strategies must be employed.

Author's Note: Parts of this chapter previously appeared in Pogrow, Stanley, "Shifting Policy Analysis and Formation from an Effectiveness to a Cost Perspective." *Educational Evaluation and Policy Analysis,* Spring 1983. Copyright 1983, American Educational Research Association, Washington, D.C.

The purpose of this chapter is to explore how technology could be used in this decade to assist educational services in delivering both traditional and technology-related skills. Technologists tend to address this issue simplistically, advocating that children be trained on computers and/or made computer-literate and assuming that everything will take care of itself. Such an approach ignores the problems and issues that accompany curricular reform—obstacles that scholars in a wide variety of disciplines have examined. The question of what constitutes an appropriate delivery system for stimulating reform has been asked in the social science literature for the past decade and a half with respect to a broad range of other policy initiatives. Such prior research is reflected extensively in the literatures of political science, evaluation, and innovation diffusion.

As a result, technology-related curricular reform should not be viewed in a conceptual vacuum. Instead, an attempt must be made to link such reform to existing knowledge about the outcomes of previous policy attempts to promote reform. This chapter will therefore explore existing social science for insights into the following questions:

(a) What are appropriate characteristics for a delivery system designed to meet the curricular challenge of changing technology if the mistakes of previous reform policy initiatives are to be avoided?
(b) Given expected levels of technological development and opportunity, what new delivery systems will become feasible during this decade?
(c) How do the characteristics of these delivery systems compare with those of the traditional one, and which system is most appropriate for promoting technology-related curricular reform?

1. A CRITIQUE OF TRADITIONAL APPROACHES TO POLICY FORMATION AND DELIVERY SYSTEMS

The major policy thrusts in education over the past decade and a half have focused on improving the effectiveness of education by shifting the distribution of educational funding in favor of compensatory services for the disadvantaged, and shifting allocation priorities to stimulate the adoption of innovative practices. The basic delivery mechanism was to use a variety of dissemination strategies for those programs and techniques that evaluation demonstrated to be effective. The dissemination strategies shifted from demonstration programs and centers to the use of linking agents and the national diffusion network concept. The grand conception was to emulate the success of the agricultural movement by adopting an R & D perspective to improve educational effectiveness (i.e., to increase the level of attainment with respect to learning outcomes). There was little concern with increasing efficiency (i.e., raising the level of attainment per unit cost, which can be accomplished by either maintaining costs while improving effectiveness or reducing costs while maintaining effectiveness).

Some argue that we have not been able to develop techniques for improving educational effectiveness and that the compensatory policies were largely failures. An increasing number of studies, however, such as Berliner (1979), Glass and Smith (1978), Miller (1981), Stallings (1975), Summers and Wolfe (1977), and Wendling and Cohen (1980), have found significant improvement effects from school-based variables and compensatory efforts. Yet, even if compensatory programs can be shown to improve the effectiveness of education, improving school effectiveness is still not realistic primary policy goal for the eighties, given:

(a) the unavailability of resources to carry out the fiscal requirements of the compensatory policies in the absence of major gains in efficiency, and

(b) the absence of adequate delivery systems for improving effectiveness.

Under the contracting fiscal conditions likely to prevail in the eighties, efficiency gains are a prerequisite for improvements in effectiveness for education as well as for General Motors. Fiscal projections like those of Kirst and Garms (1980) tend to show educational revenues unable to rise as rapidly as inflation throughout this decade. While supporters of education and advocates of special causes decry such trends and attempt to develop strategies to entice additional funding from the political process, the simple reality is that under conditions of declining societal productivity, new resources can ultimately be generated only by improved efficiency.

None of the existing methodologies for improving school effectiveness, however, currently has the potential to achieve major gains in efficiency, particularly in the delivery of higher-order and technical skills. Even when compensatory programs improve effectiveness, they do so at the expense of increased costs and therefore tend not to improve efficiency. The recent school improvement literature (e.g., Kirst, Tyack, & Hansot, 1979; Berliner, 1980) reveals major variations in terms of the amount of time that teachers and schools spend in particular activities, such as direct instruction (ranging from 46 to 90 percent of the school day), or teaching particular subject areas. Shifting the range upward to narrow the gap would indeed result in important efficiency gains. Such gains, while important, and while they can significantly improve (at least) basic skill acquisition, are constrained by the total amount of teaching time available. Therefore, the efficiency gains resulting from commonsense reallocations of teacher time, albeit valuable, are limited.

Trying to improve effectiveness under conditions of declining societal productivity is a Catch-22 wherein pursuing such policies reduces the possibility of generating the resources needed to implement the policies. Without efficiency-generated slack resources, it will be impossible to provide compensatory efforts to meet special needs, improve higher-order skills, or strengthen programs in the arts, humanities, and sciences. It will be impossible to implement any reforms, and education will continue to contract around basic services.

Another constraint on successful implementation of effectiveness enhancement policies, even where the knowledge of appropriate instructional strategies exists, is an overreliance on the transfer and utilization of information among teachers. It is difficult (nearly impossible) to find examples *in any field* of new techniques being diffused throughout a highly labor-intensive activity with fairly fixed financial incentives simply via information transfers. In those rare instances in which diffusion has succeeded in improving the quality of services and products, the knowledge diffusion was accompanied either by an economically compelling technology to reduce dependence on labor or by an increase in the capital support behind each worker. The contrast between the U.S. and USSR experiences in agriculture is a case in point. Whereas this country has been extremely successful in increasing agricultural production by combining information dissemination with the adoption of new technology, the Soviets, with their reliance on information dissemination within a structure of labor-intensive collective farming, have found it difficult to raise production, despite efforts to get farmers to adopt new techniques. If diffusing knowledge, while maintaining the labor intensity of the service (i.e., the Russian model), does not have much effect in agriculture, it is not likely to be successful in education.

There have also been shortcomings in the innovation literature, on which much of the design of delivery systems has been based. One limitation that has received a lot of attention is the presumption that adoption of an innovation is synonymous with implementation. Berman and McLaughlin (1978) and Hall and Loucks (1977) have shown that adoption and implementation are separate processes. Another problem is that researchers have assumed that if an innovation is implemented, the benefits associated with a given level of implementation are automatically transferred across sites. Despite all the work in innovation and evaluation, however, there is virtually no evidence that if district Y implements a program that has previously been demonstrated to produce learning improvement in district X, district Y will experience learning improvement (even if implementation effects are controlled for). The evaluation of the Follow-Through Program, which to date has been the only attempt to link implementation quality to learning outcomes, found large variances in results among sites that had similar degrees of implementation of the same program.

What does this mean in terms of the viability of using knowledge dissemination strategies to improve the effectiveness of schooling? First, if learning outcomes are highly independent of program implementation, there is unlikely to be any systematic effect on learning improvement from the activities of programs such as the National Diffusion Network (NDN) and the Fund for the Improvement of Postsecondary Education. These programs seek to identify and/or develop practices that work and then to disseminate them through linkage agents. The "validated" program concept of the NDN is of little utility if the benefits do not have a high probability of transferability. This issue of benefit transferability tends to be ignored by the recent evaluation of the Fund for the Improvement of Postsecondary Education (Pelavin, 1979) and by the current research on knowledge utilization and linkage agents (such as that by Emerick & Peterson, 1978). These studies focus on the diffusion of innovation or the process of attempted diffusion rather than the impact of such diffusion on student outcomes. Such studies ignore the impact of implementation activities on learning and falsely assume that the benefits of innovation are automatically transferred.

The second problem with using knowledge dissemination strategies as the primary means to improve effectiveness is this: If there are three stages of innovation diffusion (adoption, implementation, and effectiveness improvement) that operate independently, then the probability of increasing effectiveness becomes very small. For example, if the probability of the adoption of a "validated" practice is .2 and the probability of the adopted practice being successfully implemented is .2, the probability of the innovation reaching the implemented state is .04. If the probability of the implemented innovation actually improving learning in other districts is also .2, then the probability of the diffused innovation having an impact on effectiveness is only .008. Eight chances in a thousand (or 160 out of 20,000 districts experiencing increased effectiveness) is not a sufficiently high probability on which to base policy.

The probabilities are, of course, only estimates. The best available data, however, suggest that innovation adoption is an almost random event and the probability of successful implementation is extremely low. For example, Duchesneau, Cohn, and Dutton (1979) found virtually no correlation of tendencies within or between firms in the shoe industry to adopt a series of innovations. Berman and McLaughlin (1978) could find no examples ($p = 0$) of Title III innovations that were implemented once demonstration funding was withdrawn. Yin et al. (1978), on the other hand, found that 42 percent of the innovations they studied in a variety of public agencies became implemented. Yin et al. attributed the relatively high rate of implementation that they (as opposed to Berman and McLaughlin) found to the fact that the latter studied innovations of organizations process, whereas they focused on locally initiated "hard" technological innovations (i.e., those involving some sort of physical machine). Since most innovation attempts in education tend to involve externally initiated/imposed "soft" technologies (i.e., those involving a new type of social process, such as team teaching or homogeneous grouping), the Berman and McLaughlin results are more relevant and suggest that the assumption of a .2 probability for implementation is reasonable (and possibly an overestimate). A low probability for successful implementation in education is not surprising, given that many programs are couched in generalities rather than in terms of specific activities and that implementation itself depends on a series of probabilistic events related to the behavior of individuals.

The futility of depending on a strategy of information dissemination to promote implementation of innovations is probably best summed up by Knott and Wildavsky (1980):

> Dissemination is in danger of becoming a catch-all term for a series of unsupported allegations—policy relevant knowledge exists, it can be transported, a market for it is in place—and careless conclusions—what is knowledge in one place will be so in another, if only there were disseminators to connect suppliers with demanders. "Have policy will travel" may be the slogan, but as we shall see, there is reason to believe that what little knowledge there is may not travel well. (p. 540)

There are, of course, major constituencies for dissemination-based delivery systems—constituencies who argue that it is indeed possible to improve the effectiveness of dissemination strategies. The major strategies for increasing the probability of appropriate implementation behavior by individuals have been inservice and university-based training programs. The assumption has been that if individuals are given knowledge, they will apply it. The major resources expended for such training, however, seem to have had little impact on implementation quality. A case in point: Administrator training programs are dominated by efforts to train individuals to supervise and evaluate the instructional process. Such activity is indeed essential for successful implementation of new instructional efforts in the school. However, studies of the actual behavior of administrators (e.g., Blood et al., 1978) tend to find that, despite their training, administrators seldom evaluate instructional activities. In a similar vein, Berliner (1980), commenting on the cumulative impact on teaching learning theory to teachers, concludes:

> Teachers do not hold learning theories. Despite what they have been taught, they are smart enough to realize that most learning theory is bunk! (p. 125)

The extensive supervision establishment tends to respond to such criticism by arguing that a new approach to conceptualizing and teaching supervision would solve the problem. The knowledge utilization school argues that more basic research is needed to understand the conditions under which individuals apply knowledge. Common sense, however, suggests that if the knowledge dissemination effort to date, as represented by research and supervision courses, has not yet had a demonstrable impact on school effectiveness or even on administrative behavior, it is not likely to do so in the future.

A final problem with the delivery systems used in effectiveness enhancement policies relates to the nature of what is disseminated. The social process technologies that are disseminated tend to victimize rather than benefit teachers because of a failure to distinguish between "conceptual" and "physical" implementation (Pogrow, 1980). Traditional models of inservice assume that if someone understands how to do something and wants to do it (conceptual implementation), he or she will be able to, and actually will, do it (physical implementation). Traditional delivery systems and training focus on achieving conceptual implementation. Such a position ignores the possibility that individuals may not have the resources necessary to do the job. Since effectiveness-enhancing proposals tend to involve highly time-consuming social processes, traditional delivery systems usually end up in the position of pressuring teachers to engage in reforms, such as individualized instruction, for which no adequate technology exists to assist them in doing it within the constraints of the time and energy resources available to them. More often than not, the procedures that are disseminated are designed to simplify the administrator's tasks in placing additional responsibility on teachers. Herbert Simon (1971) has noted, however, that if an effectiveness-enhancement system does not simplify tasks, it tends to be ignored by the targeted individuals. As a result, a delivery system that relies on achieving conceptual implementation of typical effectiveness-improvement proposals is unlikely to result in actual implementation or improvement.

The information diffusion proposals that have the greatest potential to survive transmission through the traditional delivery system are those of the time-on-task approach to school improvement. As already indicated, these proposals have the desirable properties that (a) they view the time available to teachers as a constant and seek to reallocate it rather than increase the amount of work that must be performed, and (b) direct-instruction, time-on-task variables are very simple commonsense ones that should be easy to transmit via information diffusion.

The basic question, however, is how much improvement can be obtained solely by manipulating the simple variable of amount of instructional time allocated. Berliner (1979) estimates that anywhere from 10 to 30 percent of the variance in student outcomes (depending on the specific skill) can be explained by differences in the amount of time allocated to basic instructional processes. The questions remain, however, whether such gains, while important, are sufficient, and whether they can be obtained without involving more complex process variables such as student engagement/absorption. The gains may not be sufficient, since they are primarily limited to basic skills and offer little help in reorienting the curriculum to provide greater emphasis on technical and higher-order skills.

In addition, obtaining maximum improvement from manipulating time-on-task variables may also require increasing the level of student absorption in those tasks. Tobias (1982) argues that student absorption level is by far the most important determinant of learning. If this is true and/or teachers tend to reduce time on task when they find it impossible to maintain student engagement in given tasks, then it is also necessary to diffuse techniques to improve student absorption levels—a complex process that is unlikely to survive transmission through the traditional delivery system, for the reasons previously discussed. At this point, the policy relevance of the time-on-task approach diminishes. This does not mean that the time-on-task approach to improving school effectiveness should be ignored or that it is not important, but rather that, in its present mode of articulation, it is insufficient to meet the educational needs of a changing economy.

Effectiveness-oriented policies have large constituencies in the reform, evaluation, and supervision communities. They also have high degrees of political salability. Unfortunately, they are not likely to work, for the myriad reasons already discussed—regardless of how much money is spent for basic research. In addition, delivery systems that rely primarily on knowledge dissemination (conceptual implementation) are not likely to be effective in promoting the implementation of curricular reform.

2. APPROACHES TO POLICY FORMATION AND DELIVERY SYSTEMS

If schools are to adapt to the educational needs of changing technology, curricular offerings need to be expanded comprehensively under conditions of constrained resources and shortages of qualified personnel. Given the discussion in the previous section, the primary interventionist policy under such conditions would be to shift from effectiveness enhancement to efficiency improvement. Desired characteristics of the accompanying delivery system would be to supplement, or replace, reliance on knowledge dissemination activities with automated systems that are physically capable of providing educational services. Providing automated systems, which already embody the knowledge that would otherwise have to be disseminated, both simplifies the process of conceptual implementation and is already in a physically implemented form. As a result, the delivery process is simplified and is therefore more likely to be successful. For example, Feller, Menzel, and Engel (1974), Lambright (1977), and Yin et al. (1978) found the rate of implementation for hard technology innovation to be significantly higher than for other types of innovations in the public sector. A related goal would be to use hard technology systems to simplify the management of classroom activities.

The only way to expand the curriculum under the conditions of constrained resources likely to prevail throughout this decade is to use the very technology that is creating the need for expanded services to deliver educational services. The basic goal of such a delivery system would be to use technology to improve the efficiency with which educational services are provided by focusing on ways to reduce costs while at least maintaining existing levels of effectiveness. Technology would not be viewed as an added cost but as a substitute for labor under conditions where such substitution would not detract from student learning. The traditional mission of evaluation, to help us understand how to improve effectiveness, would be extended to provide guidance on how not to impair effectiveness.

To the extent that efficiency improvements could be made in the delivery of basic skills, resources would be freed to help schools reverse the contraction of the curriculum and to provide compensatory help, which would increase effectiveness. Slack resources could also be used to increase the technological relevance of the curriculum. Technological substitution also offers the advantage of potentially requiring a less complex delivery system for program implementation, and for providing teachers with concrete tools to simplify their implementation tasks.

The use of technology as a delivery system takes into account that education is no different from any other service in that the only way to achieve major efficiency gains is to increase the amount of self-service activities on the part of clients. Much as banks can offer more services when consumers use automated tellers, so too can more instruction be delivered per unit cost when students are engaging in instructional interactions on their own. In addition, if it is not necessary for teachers to teach all that students need to be taught, it is also not necessary to teach teachers all that schools are expected to teach. Therefore, the process of preservicing and inservicing teachers can be simplified. The latter will also reduce the dependence of delivery systems on knowledge diffusion.

Two different approaches can be used to incorporate technology into educational delivery systems. In the first, which will be referred to as a *low-leverage system,* technology is used to support and supplement the traditional activities of the teacher. Teachers coordinate the use of computers in a classroom, or a lab setting, with their own instructional activities in order to expand the amount of educational activities provided. In the second approach, which will be referred to as a *high-leverage system,* technology is used to supplant the role of the teacher. In this delivery system, educational courses and activities are delivered directly to the home or classroom without intervention by an on-site teacher.

Table 5 summarizes the differences between the traditional and the technology-based delivery systems. The next several sections describe the technology-based delivery systems in greater detail.

3. LOW-LEVERAGE DELIVERY SYSTEMS

Those who oppose the use of technology in education rightly point to the critical role teachers can play with respect to the intellectual and social development of children. A number of educational innovations, such as individualized instruction and open classrooms, sought to enhance the probability that teachers could indeed fulfill such potential. The available technologies, however, did not provide adequate means for teachers to accomplish the required tasks within the confines of the school day. As a result, classroom research, such as that of Berliner (1980) and the studies cited by Heuston (1980), tends to show that students receive virtually no individualized attention (less than one minute per day) in classroom settings. Attempts to increase the amount of individualized attention that teachers can provide students have focused on reducing the student-adult ratio. The work of Glass and Smith (1978), however, suggests that for significant learning improvements to occur, class size must be reduced to such an extent that labor-intensive approaches to increasing effectiveness are financially infeasible.

Under a low-leverage delivery system, technology would be used in the classrooms to help deliver some of the instructional activities that do not require constant teacher intervention. In other words, computers would enable students to engage in self-service learning activities much as the adult uses automated tellers. Computers would also

TABLE 5 Comparison of Delivery System Characteristics

	Traditional	Low-Leverage	High-Leverage
Primary policy goal	Improve effectiveness of traditional services	Increase service per unit of cost	Minimize cost of services provided
Secondary policy goal	Maximize use of existing networks	Improve effectiveness	Improve effectiveness
Technology used	Social contact, inservice training	Computers plus social contact	Computers plus telecommunications
Prime means of instruction	Teacher	Teacher plus computer	Telecommunicated teacher
Focus of delivery system	Conceptual implementation of reforms, i.e., teaching teachers how to do it. Transfer of social science information	Physical implementation of new services, i.e., providing an installed version, using social science to construct educational software	Physical implementation
Conception of teacher	Teacher	Teacher and manager with technological support	Inefficient form of instruction
Fundamental educational unit	School or classroom	Educational activities in classrooms	Courses

be used to assist the teacher in classroom management activities and student diagnosis. The goal would be to increase the amount of intensive educational activities available to students while freeing teachers to concentrate on those types of interactions that are uniquely human.

The issue of whether such a computer-intensive classroom is feasible is a function of the following factors: (a) technological opportunity, (b) demonstrated effectiveness, and (c) structural barriers to implementation.

Before reviewing the research evidence, it is important to note that each of these factors has different analytical properties. Technological opportunity, which represents the potential to use technology to deliver particular types of services at a given cost, is a function of time. That is, as technology progresses and costs decline, it becomes more feasible to consider using technology in a particular way. As a result, cost estimates and conclusions about technological opportunity that are reported at a point in time are relevant only to that point in time and are not relevant to the future. It is therefore impossible to assess the viability of using microcomputers in schools by examining the attempts to use the technologies of the sixties to deliver instruction.

Conclusions about the relative effectiveness (at least for maintaining learning levels) of using a certain technological approach, on the other hand, should be expected to be stable. That is, if students learn using computer-assisted instruction (CAI) delivered by a 1974 minicomputer, then similar results should be obtained using a similar CAI package on a 1985 microcomputer (at much lower cost). Structural barriers such as teacher or university resistance, however, can remain in place independent of the other two factors in the absence of appropriate policy. (Structural barriers will be discussed in detail in Chapter IV.)

Effectiveness research in conjunction with technology assessments tends to support the viability of the widespread use of technology in education during this decade with respect to the first two factors, effectiveness and technological opportunity. First of all, it appears that it is possible to use technology to deliver various forms of instructional services with resultant savings in teacher time and improved effectiveness. Much of the research has focused on the use of CAI for math basic skills, employing software developed by Pat Suppes and distributed by Computer Curriculum Corporation. Earlier reviews of the effects of CAI, such as those by Jamison, Suppes, and Wells (1974) and Jamison et al. (1976), concluded that supplementary CAI either improved or maintained previous achievement levels when it was used to replace traditional instruction at the secondary level. Glass, McGraw, and Smith (1981) estimate, on the basis of data collected from experiments in the Los Angeles Public Schools, that twenty minutes a day with math CAI can produce learning gains equivalent to reducing the pupil-teacher ratio to 2:1.

Nor are potential benefits limited to math CAI. More comprehensive research and literature reviews also find computers to offer major time savings and effectiveness improvements. Thomas (1979) concluded that CAI produces results equivalent to good instruction with respect to achievement, retention, and time required to attain mastery at the secondary level. Kulik, Kulik, and Cohen (1980), in their meta-analysis of research on computer-based instruction in higher education, found that the teacher time needed at the college level for computer-based instruction was 36 percent less than for conventional courses, with at least equal degrees of learning and affective response outcomes. A similar analysis of the effectiveness of computer-based instruction at the elementary-secondary level found that students tended to gain an average of 13 percentile points using computers as opposed to what they would have achieved using conventional approaches (Bracey, 1982, reporting on the research of Kulik et al.). Nilson (1981) has calculated that substitution of technology could reduce costs at the elementary level by 16 percent.

Research to date has tended to focus on the effectiveness and efficiency of using computers to deliver basic skill instruction. Such research, as discussed above, tends to demonstrate significant potential for substituting technology for traditional instructional interactions, particularly in math and science at the upper-elementary and secondary levels. As more sophisticated software becomes available in these and other areas, the technological opportunity for substituting technology should increase even more.

Determining technological opportunity is complicated by the lack of methodological standardization for estimating costs (Carnoy & Levin, 1975). Levin and Woo (1980) found that the current $400 per-pupil compensatory allocation could fund CAI programs for such students in only two basic skill areas. The CAI packages in that study were leased at high cost, were running on an expensive 1976 computer, and were stationed at a central location at the school with extensive environmental and retrofitting costs. The technology examined in that study does not, however, represent the current state of technological opportunity, as the same service can now be obtained using microcomputers for about one-third the cost. While the Levin and Woo study is an example of the fallacy of extending point-in-time data to another point in time, it is valuable in that it developed a standard methodology for doing point-in-time cost analyses.

Technological opportunity is clearly increasing. If a stringent criterion of $50 to $200 per pupil is used, it is feasible at present to use computers only in centers to deliver basic skill instruction in a variety of content areas. (Such costs are considered reasonable for significant amounts of technological substitution, since they are half of existing compensatory program costs and are recoverable with increases in teacher-pupil ratios of only 1-4 students per teacher.) Because of the expected continuing evolution of hardware and software, low-leverage systems that can deliver a combination of basic and higher-order skills at the classroom level will be feasible by 1985 (see Appendix A for a cost analysis). It may also be possible by that time to have labs for the same unit cost using computer-controlled video disk systems with highly advanced forms of instructional software.

Advances in artificial intelligence provide the potential for more sophisticated versions of educational software, hereafter referred to as intelligent CAI. Such computer packages will perform higher-level cognitive interactions with students. Brown et al. (1978), for example, have developed an experimental package that is better than teachers in diagnosing the cause of student errors in math calculations. A number of easy-to-use programming languages have been developed that facilitate educational interaction with computers, even by preschoolers. Examples include Smalltalk, developed by Allan Kay, and LOGO, by Seymour Papert. The latter is already available for microcomputers, whereas the former will probably not be feasible on low-cost computers until around mid-decade.

It can also be expected that the supply and quality of conventional instructional software will increase. Most of the major educational publishing houses are beginning to produce courseware and a wide variety of drill and practice exercises for microcomputers. Several companies are now starting to produce logic skill training software as well as software that helps develop skills in a variety of technical areas. R & D programs are now under way at a number of universities (e.g., MIT, Utah State University, and the University of Nebraska) to produce software for computer-controlled video disk machines.

Hardware is also continuing to evolve. More powerful microcomputers should be available around mid-decade for half the cost of present systems. An inexpensive computer-controlled video disk system (around $1,200) should also be available by that time.

Since the technological opportunity for using computer-intensive classrooms to deliver a wide range of skills is projected to be feasible by the 1985-87 period, such a delivery system can be considered a viable policy option for the expected public demands and needs for comprehensive curricular reform. (The research implications of developing such delivery systems are explored in Chapter VI.) High-leverage systems, on the other hand, will probably not be feasible on a large scale until later in the decade or early in the 1990s.

4. HIGH-LEVERAGE DELIVERY SYSTEMS

The advantage of high-leverage efficiency strategies is that they minimize the political dislocations within education that could result from large-scale technological substitution. The low-leverage approach involves a tradeoff between efficiency and effectiveness concerns; i.e., there is no attempt to maximize potential efficiency gains. High-leverage delivery systems seek to maximize potential cost, maintaining (at least) existing levels of learning effectiveness. This form of delivery system seeks to minimize the ratio between the number of people required to deliver educational services and the number of people served. Two basic types of high-leverage strategies can be envisioned: (a) home-based and (b) school- or community-center based.

Under a futures scenario in which societal productivity and available fiscal resources continue to decline, if teachers refuse to cooperate with low-leverage strategies, and/or the needed classroom technological support does not surface rapidly enough, large segments of society might begin to demand high-leverage technological substitution strategies to reduce costs and taxes. Such delivery systems could also appear spontaneously as increasing numbers of parents begin voluntarily to use in-home educational technology as an alternative, or supplement, to the cost of private schools.

The prototype of the successful high-leverage system is *Sesame Street*. Schramm (1977) and Jamison et al. (1978) have demonstrated the cost-effectiveness of high-leverage media such as radio and television. The major educational limitation of these media, however, is that they do not provide the opportunity for interactive responses. New technologies that will permit simple two-way interaction (i.e., multiple-choice responses) are becoming available via satellite and cable telecommunications to both home and school. QUBE is an example of such a system. As computers become more prevalent in the home, more complex interactions will become possible. An alternative to total dependence on telecommunications for high-leverage systems is the distribution of educational courses on video disks. *As technology evolves, highly leveraged delivery systems will begin to offer the same interactive opportunities as will be available from low-leverage delivery systems* (although this point will probably not be reached until the latter part of this decade).

Madden (1981) notes an example of the potential of highly leveraged technological delivery systems:

> Considering productivity in education with respect to videotex, one can compare professors sitting in a room with a hundred or so people against thousands accessing educational routines at their own convenience from their own homes—augmented in many cases by video programs over TV channels or possibly video cassettes or video disks. (p. 260)

The educational establishment has only recently begun to take notice of the potential of cable systems. *Education USA* (1980) describes the successful use of cable (in a low-leveraged manner) by one school district and provides useful guidance to school administrators on how to leverage the competition among cable companies to make sure that adequate cable capabilities are available for education. Although there has been no discussion within the establishment of providing highly leveraged educational services via cable, the Walter Annenberg donation to the Public Broadcasting Service may provide the means and incentive for such an effort to begin.

The distinction between home- and school-based delivery systems is not a trivial one from a policy perspective. While Chapters VI and VII deal with policy issues in detail, it is important to note that home-based, high-leverage strategies raise some critical equity issues in terms of access to the services. Access issues are not, however, limited to home services. The access of school libraries to electronic data bases also presents challenging policy concerns.

5. COMPOSITE DELIVERY SYSTEMS

While distinctions have been made between various forms of delivery systems, it should be noted that they can be intertwined. The basic unit of consideration is not the form of delivery system but the educational activities themselves, some of which can be delivered via traditional or low-leverage techniques, others via high-leverage techniques. In addition, a common component of each of the new delivery systems may constitute a new type of delivery system in itself: the *self-delivery* component. It should be possible by mid-decade for consumers to purchase computers and video disk systems for $500 along with extensive educational software, for either device, for an additional $200. Low-cost adapters for cable and satellite reception, as well as interfaces between video disk and computer, will also be widely available around that time. These devices will make it possible to broadcast educational services into the home on either a regional or a worldwide basis. As such services become available, increasing numbers of educational institutions may begin to award credit for subjects learned via home technology upon demonstration of competence.

It can also be anticipated that, if appropriate policies (such as those recommended in Chapters VI and VII) are followed, there will be increasing availability of software to match the hardware capabilities. Some of the software will contain the advanced features that make self-teaching possible. In addition, the scope of the available software will increase dramatically. Entire courses in math and science will be available—for both school and home. Table 7 contains projections of the availability of technological potentials in education.

The availability of composite forms of delivery systems has several structural implications for delivering educational services. First, the developing self-service capability will mean that, for the first time, clients will have increasing alternatives to complete dependence on the public schools for the education of their children, even if voucher proposals are not passed. For example, Papert (1980) has suggested that

> the computer presence will enable us to so modify the learning environment outside the classrooms so that much if not all the knowledge schools try to teach with such pain and expense and such limited success will be learned, as the child learns to talk, painlessly, successfully, and without organized instruction. (p. 9)

The second fundamental structural change made possible by the availability of composite delivery systems is that, for the first time, the variety of educational services a given institution will be able to provide will be largely independent of institutional size. This will be true for small private schools as well as public ones. The political and policy implications of these two factors will be explored in the remaining chapters of this book.

6. SUMMARY

Technology is making new forms of delivery systems feasible during this decade. Given the limitations of traditional forms of delivery systems, it is unlikely that they will be adequate to support either the interventionist policy goal of increasing school effectiveness or the curricular expansion and innovation needed to provide the educational skills the new technology requires. This is particularly true under the condition of constrained resources, which is likely to prevail throughout this decade. Achieving the goals of educational quality during the eighties will, therefore, require a growing dependence on the new forms of delivery systems, particularly the low-leverage and composite delivery systems that will be available by around mid-decade.

A number of factors, however, may impede the use of the alternative delivery systems in public education. The impediments, as well as the likely consequences of failing to use the new delivery systems, will be explored in the next chapter.

ENVIRONMENTAL COLLAPSE
IV
Projected Consequences if Public Schools Do Not Respond to Technological Needs

IF PUBLIC DEMANDS for technology-related services increase around mid-decade as predicted, and if the technological opportunity to provide such services (using nontraditional delivery systems) also develops around that time, are public schools likely to respond? What are the likely consequences if they do not? This section will explore the answers to these questions.

1. STRUCTURAL BARRIERS TO AN ADEQUATE RESPONSE

Existing literature tends to identify a number of structural barriers that are likely to impede the large-scale use of technology in the public schools. The following are the most prominently cited barriers:

(a) inadequate capital resources for schools to purchase computers;
(b) no incentives for teachers to use computers;
(c) lack of computer literacy among current teachers and administrators;
(d) shortages of teachers with technical backgrounds;
(e) shortages of graduates with technical majors entering education;
(f) political resistance by teacher unions;
(g) lack of incentives, or profit opportunities, for industry to develop educational software;

87

   (h) inadequate protection against software piracy;

   (i) lack of qualified faculty in colleges of education to offer quality pre-
and inservice training to personnel in the application of technology;
and

   (j) lack of knowledge about the uses and importance of technology on the
part of governmental officials.

It is difficult to project the future impact of each of these factors.
The two key limiting factors to the utilization of technology in education are probably the availability of software and the ability, as well as
the willingness, of existing personnel to work with the new forms of
technology. With respect to the former factor, there has been a recent
rapid increase in the amount of software available—particularly instructional games, math CAI, and a variety of elementary-grade curricular material. A lot of new small software companies are emerging,
while the large book publishers are hedging their bets by producing
software that emulates their books. While the latter software does not
represent the state of the art, it has the virtue (from the perspective of
the publishers) of requiring minimal investment.

Although it is fashionable to point out the high cost of producing
software (cost estimates usually range from $30,000 to $100,000 for
an hour of quality instructional material), such statistics are mislead-
ing in the context of evolving technology. As low-cost computers, programmers, and program development aids proliferate, new entrepreneurs can be expected to enter the business of developing educational
software, a business for which the capital requirements and development time are declining.

The primary software problem is that much of the material developed in the future is not likely to contain new, creative, instructional
approaches. Most existing software is oriented to drill and practice.
Developing more intelligent software that is capable of understanding
and remediating student learning problems and of teaching abstract
concepts in a highly automated way will require a large R & D investment. The private sector is not, however, likely to make such an investment at present, because of the difficulty in preventing software
piracy in existing floppy disk technology. Piracy would depress the

size of the potential market for educational software, which at this time is already small. Market Data Retrieval (1982) has estimated the size of this market to be a paltry $12 million.

The educational software market should, however, begin to expand rapidly as companies such as CBS and Mattel start marketing instructional software to the home. The piracy problem should decline around mid-decade, as new, more secure alternatives for storing programs, such as video disks and high-density ROM (read-only memory) chips become available. From that point in time, however, even if the size of the potential software market is increasing sufficiently to warrant large R & D investments, it would still take private industry an additional four to five years to produce the more advanced forms of software voluntarily. In the absence of government intervention, the advanced forms of software that are needed and are technically feasible might not be available until the end of the decade (at the earliest).

In addition to software problems, major personnel problems limit the ability of schools to respond to the educational demands of the information economy. First are the tremendous shortages of qualified math and science teachers in virtually every school system in the United States. Guthrie and Zussman (1982) note estimates that 22 percent of all secondary math positions either are not filled or are filled by individuals not certified to teach math, and that the Los Angeles Unified School District alone is going to need 600 additional math teachers in 1983. The study goes on to note that, in 1982, only one student was enrolled in the math teacher education program, and five in science education, at the 30,000-student campus of the University of California at Berkeley. According to the National Council of Teachers of Mathematics, 50 percent of the new math teachers hired in recent years were (and probably still are) unqualified, and there has been a 77 percent decline in the number of new secondary math teachers prepared since 1977 (Education Commission of the States, 1982).

There are also shortages in higher education: a 10 percent shortfall in the number of faculty needed in engineering, and 16 percent in computer science (Main, 1982a). The shortages would be worse without the increased use of faculty from foreign countries. Such shortages are likely to get worse, since the numbers of students earning Ph.D.s in engineering and computer science have declined 33 and 45 percent respectively during the previous decade (Simon & Grant, 1972; Vance & Eiden, 1981). In addition, American students represent a declining percentage of those who do attain Ph.D.s in these fields.

The lack of interest among college students with technical skills to become teachers comes at a time when estimates of the number of math and science teachers leaving education each year range from 17,000 to 25,000 (Guthrie & Zussman, 1982). The growing critical shortage is a result of a combination of factors, including (a) significantly higher salaries in industry, (b) better working conditions in industry, and (c) the tendency of districts facing declining enrollment to fire newer teachers regardless of their fields. Nor is it likely that it will be possible to retrain sufficient numbers of existing teachers in overcrowded subject areas to become effective math and science teachers, because of a general decline in teacher ability. Victor and Schlechty (1982) found that not only do a disproportionate number of low-academic-ability students enter teaching, but they are also more likely to remain in teaching than the high-academic-ability individuals who do enter teaching. Indeed, this study found that over 80 percent of the high-ability teachers, or teacher candidates, left teaching. Over time, this trend reduces the potential pool of individuals who can switch into technical areas and teach effectively.

In an era of constrained resources, the only practical way to counter these personnel problems is to enlist technology in delivering instruction in the technical areas. Acceptance of the new technology by teachers, administrators, and unions, however, remains to be seen. There has been a recent spate of grass-roots interest in technology among educational professionals, and educators at all levels are seeking to acquire knowledge in technology use. This interest is reflected in high attendance at microcomputer institutes and the rash of new technology journals (five in the past year) aimed at educators who do not have technical backgrounds. In 1982, major professional associations began to feature technology-related sessions at their annual conventions. Likewise, publications of the professional organizations have started to include increasing numbers of articles on technology.

The motivation for practitioners to engage in such self-learning activities ranges from professional growth to gauging the feasibility of pursuing a career in technology outside education. Whether these self-learning activities will continue and attract a significant percentage of existing educators, whether such training will provide adequate technical skills to enable the "typical" teacher to manage a "computer-rich classroom environment," whether those who do acquire such skills will stay in education, and whether the availability of such learning opportunities will overcome biases against change all remain to be seen. Also uncertain is the overall quality of the instructional opportunities and information that will be provided. It is unlikely (though not impossible) that the typical college of education will be able to offer substantial amounts of high-quality training in technology, given the inertial commitment to traditional kinds of programs and delivery systems.

What is fairly certain is that it will be impossible for education to fulfill its need for technical people by attracting outsiders to the profession, given the overall shortage of such individuals (which bids up their value to the private sector), the uniform salary structure of education, and the unattractiveness of many aspects of education work (e.g., hall patrol and bathroom duty).

2. PROJECTIONS OF PUBLIC SCHOOL RESPONSE

Because of software and personnel problems, as well as the expected political and cultural opposition to change within the education profession, most policy studies tend to be highly pessimistic about the widespread adoption of new technology in education. Nilles et al. (1980) estimate that the penetration of microcomputers into the school will be only a *sixteenth* of the equivalent figure for home use by 1990. A recent survey by the National Center for Education Statistics found only 30,000 microcomputers in the schools for instructional purposes as of fall 1980. Walling, Thomas, and Larson (1979) were also pessimistic about the ability of schools to adopt. They concluded that "the major impacts . . . will not be in the school, but probably in the home" (p. 4). They noted that computers would most likely be found in homes where there simultaneously exists a high regard for education and a dissatisfaction with the public schools.

The analyses of these studies are, however, quite "soft" and may prove to be grossly inaccurate (in either direction). The present willingness of individuals to engage in self-learning activities and the emergence of software-development entrepreneurs may mitigate the pessimistic projections of technological adoption by the public schools. Indeed, recent estimates tend to be somewhat more optimistic. Market Data Retrieval (1982) projects that the market for school computers will grow to $145 million in 1985 (from $35 million in 1980). The National Center for Educational Statistics estimates that the number of microcomputers in the schools tripled between 1980 and 1982 (to 96,000), and a survey by Quality Education Data, Inc., a marketing firm, found that 46 percent of schools had micros by 1982.

Unfortunately, statistics on the sale of microcomputers to schools tell very little about the extent to which schools are adapting to the educational needs of the information economy. Information on the number of computers in schools tells as much about quality of education, the degree to which new computer-use skills are being taught, or the extent to which higher-order skill training is being provided as statistics on the number of toilets available to students. The real questions are (a) How are computers that are being placed in the school being used to modify and expand the curriculum for the majority of students? (b) Have the computers become the sole province of the math teachers and the very bright students? (c) Does the school have any plan or idea for using computers to improve learning outcomes for the majority of students? and (d) Are the computers being used strictly to make students aware of what the computer can do, or are they being used to provide students with higher-order and technical skills? The answers to these questions will provide the statistics for determining whether schools are adapting their curricula to meet the educational needs imposed by the new economic realities.

It therefore appears that while pessimistic projections of computer use in the schools predominate, it is really impossible at this point to predict the response. Nor can the commonly used statistic of the number of computers in the school be considered a reliable yardstick of whether schools are responding to the educational needs being generated by the information economy. What can be predicted with more certainty, however, are the likely consequences if the public school response to the expected demands for more technologically relevant curricula is inadequate.

3. POLITICAL CONSEQUENCES

Since access to knowledge about technology will increasingly become a primary work prerequisite, it can be anticipated that there will be strong public dissatisfaction if the public schools fail to provide such training. Traditional conceptions of political process would predict that such dissatisfaction will translate into political activism. Can the public schools use existing political buffers to survive external political activism generated by their failure to become technologically relevant?

The many case studies in the implementation and decision-making literature (e.g., Sabatier, 1978) chronicle examples of organizations successfully resisting rational external input yet continuing to thrive. Schools and their unions score impressively on traditional measures of political power. Traditional theories of political process would tend to predict that public schools could (if they chose to do so) resist the pressure to become technologically relevant without having to make substantial changes.

Traditional theories of political process, such as that of Easton (1965), focus on the efforts of outsiders to modify the internal decision-making core of organizations. Pogrow (1981) has, however, hypothesized that the primary force impinging on education in the eighties will not be external activism but rather *environmental collapse.* Environmental collapse is a process wherein dissatisfied constituents do not try to change an organization. Instead, they abandon it for an alternative, economically compelling service or product made possible by a fundamentally new technology. Historical examples of politically dominant groups and organizations that became victims of environmental collapse include scribes, artisans, ocean liners, and the Pony Express. More recent examples are the loss of domestic market dominance by U.S. automakers and the failure of the U.S. Postal Service to obtain its political objective to control electronic mail.

Education is not as likely to be immune from environmental collapse in this decade as it was in the past. If technology can reduce the cost of providing a number of educational services and can expand the number of services offered independent of institutional size, small private schools will be able to offer a comprehensive curriculum at a lower cost differential (relative to public schools) than at present. Tuition tax credits would further narrow this differential. As the cost of private education declines, it becomes a viable option for an increasing number of individuals. Under a conception of environmental collapse, as new technologies for sharing and communicating knowledge become even more economically compelling, new forms of education and educational institutions will develop, and demand for these services will increase—regardless of whether public schools change to a more technologically relevant and efficient form. If public schools do not adjust the nature of the educational services they deliver and how they deliver them, the utilization of the alternatives by substantial segments of the population will reduce or eliminate the political and monopolistic advantages currently enjoyed by the public schools.

A limited form of environmental collapse may already be occurring in institutions of higher education in the form of what Pogrow (1981) has termed academic flight. Academic flight refers to a process wherein graduate students and faculty in fields such as engineering and computer science, where technology is progressing rapidly, voluntarily leave academia to work in industry. While industry offers higher salaries, the availability of more modern equipment for engaging in research and learning seems to be an even more critical factor (National Science Foundation & Department of Education [NSF-DOE], 1981). As previously noted, the NSF-DOE task force estimated that engineering schools underinvested in new capital equipment by $700 million during the past decade. In addition, many students in the technical areas leave earlier than they used to because of the often correct perception that they have already learned what they need to know and/or what the institution is capable of teaching them. Both Apple and Microsoft (one of the largest microcomputer software companies) were formed by college dropouts.

There appears to be little that universities can do to reverse the trend of faculty and students in key technical areas voluntarily leaving academia. If this trend continues, it will erode the university's ability to attract fiscal resources as the locus of knowledge-generation activities shifts away, regardless of how much political power the universities possess. What seems to be happening is that the conversion of industry to information work is modifying some of the historical environmental boundaries and interrelationships between industry and university, and it is occurring in the fields where knowledge is progressing most rapidly.

At the other end of the spectrum, elementary-secondary education is losing its market share of basic skills training as industry (Hymowitz, 1981) and the military greatly expand their efforts in that area. Main (1982b) reports that the United States already spends $40 billion for job training outside the educational system. While this is currently not a form of environmental collapse, it does suggest a possible mechanism for it. If in the likely event that the new organizations providing basic, or technology-use-related, skills develop a better replicable technology for doing it, then its adoption by private schools could increase their rate of growth—which *is* a form of environmental collapse. For example, the success of private summer computer camps could lead to private computer schools.

It should be emphasized that environmental collapse is a relatively rare phenomenon in the era of large bureaucracies. The probability of its significantly impacting education in this decade is closely linked to the accuracy of the technology assessment made in Chapter I. There is probably, however, enough truth in that section to convince us not to rely on the simple belief that what was true in the past will be true in the future or that existing scholarly traditions are adequate to predict the political dynamics that are likely to occur.

4. CONCEPTIONS OF ENVIRONMENTAL COLLAPSE

Instead of abandoning public schools for private ones, environmental collapse could take another form: the abandonment of schools in favor of high-leverage home-based delivery systems. Such a response is, however, unlikely, given the socialization functions of schooling and the increasing number of single-parent and dual-wage-earner families.

The more likely effect of the availability of home-delivered services will be that the number of children obtaining basic skills instruction in the home will increase, and parents will expect schools to provide more creative learning and socialization activities. Mattel Electronics is already marketing instructional software to the home, and its advertisements promise parents that the product will make their children smarter in sixty days. It is not clear whether public schools that have spent half a decade contracting around the provision of basic skills would be able to respond with a more creative curriculum. Failure to do so, however, will result in a major loss of credibility with the public, who will be discovering that they can establish self-paced, individualized programs for their own children at home and that children can learn substantial amounts in a self-service mode. Once this realization dawns, it will be difficult for public schools that do not incorporate such techniques to hide behind a shield of professional expertise or convince taxpayers to support highly inefficient modes of delivering instruction.

The availability of home systems could result in a different form of environmental collapse at the senior high school level. The opportunity for individuals to engage in self-service learning activities at home could lead to a reduced willingness on the part of taxpayers to support both four years of high school and comprehensive higher education. This could result in a reduction in the number of years of schooling required for entry into the workplace or higher education— a partial form of environmental collapse.

Regardless of the particular way environmental collapse may manifest itself, it is unlikely that public schools will be able to ignore the need to become more technologically relevant without a substantial loss in credibility, importance, and enrollment. Educators cannot ignore the changing environment and count on their political buffers to protect them; nor can political scientists assume that political activism is the only recourse available to the public.

5. IMPLICATIONS FOR POLICY AND PRACTICE

Can public schools overcome the structural barriers that would otherwise prevent them from adapting to the new educational needs of the changing environment? Will public schools respond with comprehensive curricular reform and use nontraditional delivery systems in the process? While it is fascinating to speculate on the answers to these questions and it is intellectually chic to answer no, it is really impossible to answer with any degree of certainty. Nor are these the really important questions from the perspective of policy and practice. What is important is (a) describing in detail what would constitute an appropriate response on the part of public education and (b) determining the types of policies that could and should be pursued at the local, state, and federal levels to reduce the impact of the structural barriers to such a response.

It appears that the failure of public schools to overcome the structural barriers would result in a proliferation of private alternatives that take advantage of the capabilities of technology to help deliver educational services at lower cost. It also appears, however, that it is in the public interest to maintain a public educational system of reasonable quality to facilitate social integration and equal opportunity. In addition, allowing structural barriers to reform to persist (particularly the inadequate supplies of intelligent software) could reduce the overall effectiveness of the private technology-based alternatives that would emerge as well as limit the potential improvement of the public system. It is therefore important to consider policies that can overcome the barriers by that point in time when technological opportunity will make it feasible to provide substantial alternative instruction. Delineating such policies at all governmental levels will be the primary focus of the remaining chapters.

6. SUMMARY

The first part of this book has focused on what technology-related societal changes are occurring and what types of curricular reform will be necessitated by such changes. It is projected that public schools must be ready to respond by 1985-87 if they are not to suffer environmental collapse. At the same time, a number of structural barriers (some of which are not under the control or the responsibility of public education) are likely to prevent the public schools from adapting.

The second half of this book focuses on addressing the issues of (a) what constitutes an appropriate response on the part of public education if it is to respond to the new educational needs and demands and (b) what kinds of policies are needed at all levels of government if the structural barriers to such response are to be overcome.

V

DEFINING APPROPRIATE USES OF COMPUTERS IN EDUCATION

WHILE IT IS NOT CERTAIN that public schools will be able to avoid the problem of environmental collapse—or even that they will be interested in trying—the question remains as to what would constitute appropriate policies and practices for districts that want to establish a technologically relevant curriculum by the 1985-87 period. Indeed, what is a technologically relevant curriculum, and what constitutes appropriate use of computers in schools? This chapter will attempt to answer these questions for a low-leverage delivery system.

1. CONCEPTIONS OF THE ROLES OF COMPUTERS

There are varying perceptions of the roles of computers in the school. Some groups are totally opposed to the introduction of computers into the schools, believing they are a fad or part of a plot by an elite group to impose a uniform national curriculum on schools. Some supporters of technology also oppose the use of computers in schools because they feel that (a) the technology is changing too rapidly to allow prudent decisions at this juncture and/or (b) that the current generation of hardware is not yet sufficiently powerful to run intelligent software (which doesn't exist anyway) and that the educational value of existing software is extremely limited. At the other end of the spectrum are the advocates, who support a variety of often conflicting agendas. These agendas include (a) training a select group of students to be computer scientists; (b) training all students to be computer scientists (a reincarnation of the new math disaster, wherein mathematicians decided that the highly abstract reasoning activities they themselves found fascinating should transfer to all students); (c) training most students only in the basic operation of computers; (d) using computers primarily to teach basic skills; (e) using computers primarily to teach subjects, or to provide educational experiences, that would otherwise not be available; (f) training most teachers to write computer programs, or at least to develop their own computer curricular materials using authoring languages such as PILOT; and/or (g) using computers to replace or reduce the number of teachers.

These varying perspectives and agendas are confusing to practitioners, most of whom do not yet have sufficient experience to form their own opinions. The three most common practitioner responses to this dilemma are (a) to do nothing, (b) to buy computers as a public relations ploy (i.e., issue a press release bragging about how many new computers have been purchased in order to co-opt community pressure for computer use), or (c) to establish a computer literacy program. The problem with the last two options is that they usually do not relate the acquisition of equipment to any systematic set of educational objectives. The computer literacy response usually consists of providing students with limited low-grade computer use activities, such as learning to turn the computer on and off and getting some experience using a few programs. This direct experience is usually supplemented by providing students with information about computers. From the perspective of the administrator, isolating the computer component of the curriculum into a single, low-activity type of course or experience called "computer literacy" has the virtue of being a low-cost, easily scheduled solution to the problem of developing a technologically relevant curriculum. Such a solution also has the administrative virtue of minimizing disruption to the rest of the curriculum.

The computer-literacy solution, however, hardly seems adequate for responding to the types of problems and challenges previously described. In addition, such a solution also ignores the capability of the computer to deliver a wide range of curricular services. What, then, constitutes appropriate linkages between curriculum and computer use in schools?

2. CRITERIA FOR DETERMINING APPROPRIATE USES

The first step in conceptualizing what is meant by appropriate use of computers (or any technology) in schools is to define the implications of the availability and use of that technology in society as a whole for modifying the existing curriculum. What skills must education now impart in order to serve the needs of the technologies that society is likely to adopt on a large scale? An educational system that meets these demands will be said to provide a *technologically relevant curriculum*. In the case of computers and their attendant technologies, there are specific technical skills associated with their use that the majority of the population will need to apply (to varying extents and degrees of sophistication) and that are not part of the traditional curriculum of the schools. Such skills include word processing, computer repair, programming, and communications networking.

Providing specific technology use skills is not, however, sufficient for technological relevance. As already noted, in an age in which tons of information can be generated or accesssed in a split second, critiquing, synthesizing, analyzing, and applying such information creatively will displace the more routine aspects of substantial portions of white- and blue-collar work. It is therefore crucial that schools stimulate greater degrees of higher-order skills among a broader range of students. Although the teaching of higher-order skills is theoretically part of the traditional curriculum, the national assessment data already cited indicate that higher-order skills are a reality for a shrinking minority of public school students. The failure of the schools in the seventies to adopt any of the special curricula that were developed to stimulate creativity, combined with the prevalence of highly structured tracking systems, reinforces the view that public schools currently make little effort to promulgate higher-order skills among the majority of their students, or that whatever effort they do make are largely ineffectual.

Whether improving the level and distribution of higher-order skills is viewed as a new technology-related curricular initiative or a component of improving the effectiveness of the traditional curriculum, it will be impossible to improve higher-order skills without also improving traditional basic skills. The development of a technologically relevant curriculum is thus inextricably linked to traditional goals of school improvement. Therefore, the improvement of higher-order skills is probably best conceived as a goal that is common to both school improvement and technological relevance, a relationship that is depicted in Figure A. As a result of this relationship, the following general goals of computer use will be considered "appropriate" for schools:

(a) Computers should be used to provide technology use skills to the majority of students.
(b) Computers should be used as a delivery system to improve school effectiveness (with regard to both basic and higher-order skills) in a manner consistent with research findings, in order to ensure that *such use is limited to circumstances wherein it will be cost-effective.* (While this concern with improving school effectiveness seems to contradict the argument in Chapter III that policymakers should shift their concerns from effectiveness to efficiency-oriented policies, in reality what is being proposed are efficiency enhancement policies. Rather than producing efficiency for the sake of efficiency, however, the goal is to maximize the efficiency-enhancement capabilities of technology in a *systematic* way so as also to raise effectiveness.)

While the first goal is self-explanatory, the second is more ambiguous in the absence of specification as to how computers could be linked to school effectiveness. The obvious way to conceive this linkage is under circumstances where students learning on a computer achieve higher scores than would have been expected with traditional instruction. The research cited in Chapter III suggests that this outcome is more likely to occur in math than in reading, and at the upper-elementary and high school grade levels rather than in early elementary grades. Using computers to deliver instruction and practice in math would thus be an example of an application that produces direct learning gains. Direct gains will thus be considered the first criterion for appropriate computer use for effectiveness improvement.

The current work on school improvement and the microeconomics of increasing effectiveness suggest a second, less traditional way of linking the use of technology to criteria of effectiveness. These schools of thought, as represented by the work of Stallings (1975) and Berliner (1980), essentially view the educational process as a series of transactions between students and teachers in classrooms. The key to

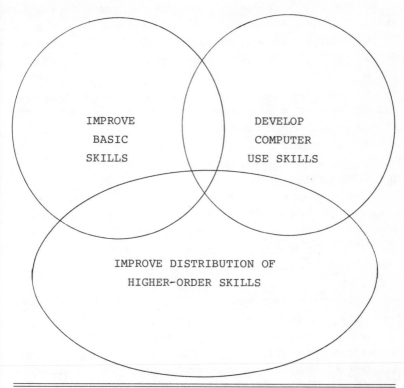

FIGURE A   Interrelationship of Basic, Higher-Order, and Computer Use Skills

improving school effectiveness is viewed by these research traditions as increasing the amount of direct-instruction transactions provided in the classroom per unit time. (This line of research will be discussed in greater detail in Chapter VI.) Therefore, whatever time technology can save a teacher in delivering a particular set of instructional tasks creates the potential for a net increase in the time allocated to instruction. The time-on-task research suggests that such an increase will result in improved effectiveness if teachers and administrators use the technology-generated time saved to increase the amount of time they spend on other instructional tasks. Thus, the second criterion of appropriate effectiveness-related computer use is *the extent to which a particular application can save personnel time by automating the delivery of a set of instructional transactions so that personnel may increase the time they devote to other tasks.*

Automation is defined as a net reduction in the number of instructional transactions that personnel must administer and supervise because students are able to use technology to obtain the instruction in a self-service mode. Instructional automation can occur in many forms, ranging from complex activities (such as individualizing the presentation of original curricular material) to more prosaic, but time-consuming, ones (such as checking compositions for spelling errors). Although automation can have only an indirect/potential impact on school improvement (since personnel must use the additional time wisely), it is included in the proposed model because its effects are potentially great.

Finally, appropriateness, the cost-effectiveness dimension of applications that do not improve effectiveness but reduce costs without impairing effectiveness, should also be considered. As a result, the third criterion of appropriate effective computer use is *the extent to which a computerized application can reduce costs without impairing learning.*

The differences among the three effectiveness criteria are illustrated in Figure B. Assume that funds are available to support the delivery of either six instructional transactions by a teacher, or five by a teacher and three by technology, related to two learning objectives. Diagram #1 describes the traditional approach, which produces learning outcomes at levels X and Y for learning objectives A and B respectively. Under the first criterion of effectiveness enhancement for technology use (Diagram #2), technology has been used to provide a net increase in instructional transactions for learning objective B, which has resulted in directly improving the degree of learning (to level Y′) for that objective. In Diagram #3, technology has been used to reduce substantially the personnel time required to deliver instructional task B by two-thirds, and has thus made it possible to increase the amount of teacher-delivered services relative to objective A, with a consequential performance improvement in level X′. In Diagrams #4A and 4B, there have been neither improvement nor impairment in the learning outcomes, but the number of transactions that personnel must provide have been reduced, resulting in either a net cost-saving or a shift in available personnel time to provide instruction for a new objective, thus resulting in a net expansion of the curriculum for the same cost.

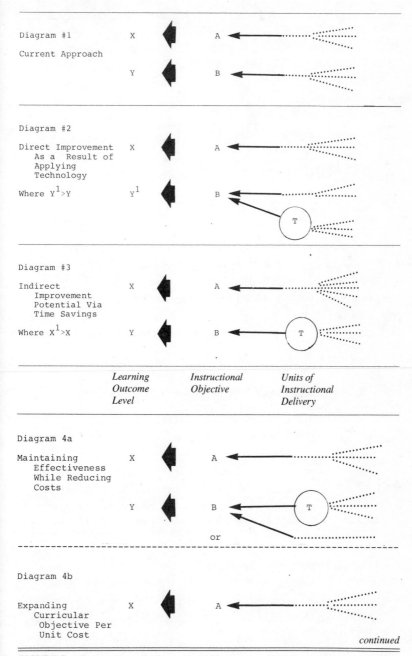

FIGURE B   Comparison of Alternative Effectiveness Criteria

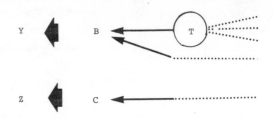

Where ⓣ indicates the use of technology to deliver instructional
units .... Instructional interactions

FIGURE B (Continued)

Decisions about which modes of effectiveness enhancement are
most appropriate for which instructional objectives need to be made
on the basis of research findings and common sense. Although existing research (largely produced during the minicomputer era) can provide significant help in determining the types of transactions for
which technology can substitute, a great deal more is needed (as discussed in Chapter 6).

3. A MODEL FOR ANALYZING APPROPRIATENESS

Based on the discussion in the previous section, *the model that will
be proposed for guiding practice and research in choosing appropriate uses of computers in schools relates the curricular components to
the three effectiveness-enhancement criteria.* The curricular components for which computer use will be considered appropriate are (a)
basic skills, (b) higher-order cognitive skills, and (c) technology-specific skills. Computer use activities are considered effectiveness-enhancing if they

(a) directly improve learning outcomes,
(b) create the potential for improving effectiveness by reducing the
    amount of personnel time that would otherwise be required for deliv-
    ering a given activity (so that more instruction can be provided for a
    different objective), and
(c) reduce the costs of a set of instructional transactions without impair-
    ing effectiveness.

In order to avoid overlap between categories b and c, category c will refer to cost-savings other than those associated with reductions in personnel or personnel time allocations. Rather, category c will refer to savings made possible by reductions in capital plant and equipment requirements.

The proposed model considers a computer application appropriate if it is used to deliver technology-specific skills or if it meets one of the effectiveness-enhancement criteria for delivery of instruction relative to one of the other curricular components. Table 6 illustrates the application of the proposed model to some of the more common modes of computer use. Research cannot at this time unambiguously place all the reviewed uses in appropriate cells. Question marks are used to indicate those cases in which it is not clear whether the usage in a given cell is appropriate. For example, although one would expect that the use of simulations would increase basic skill and higher cognitive skill learning, it has not yet been conclusively shown to do so. At the same time, Glenn, Gregg and Tipple (1982) found that successful use of simulations requires the teacher to engage in extensive, sophisticated class preparation and debriefing activities. As a result, most simulations cannot be viewed as potential time-reduction tools (appropriateness criterion b), but there may be a direct improvement application (criterion a).

Some simulations, however, can reduce costs (criterion c). For example, simulations for driver education and science laboratory experiments can replace expensive capital equipment.

Computer use, at its best, results in both reductions in personnel time and direct improvements in effectiveness. Math CAI is the classic example of such an application. At the other end of the spectrum is computer-managed instruction (CMI, used here to refer to computer programs that diagnose student problems and then suggest remedial strategies and/or programs, which track student progress across an array of objectives). Bozeman (1979) found no evidence that CMI improves student achievement. Moreover, the reams of output produced by the system, which administrators find impressive, do not reduce teacher time requirements. Quite the opposite. Digesting and implementing all the implications of the printout requires an enormous amount of additional teacher time. Such an expansion of time is viewed as undesirable by the model, regardless of how worthy the

TABLE 6   Model for Determining Appropriateness of Computer Applications

Does Application Save Personnel Time?	Does Application Have Direct Impact on Increasing Basic Skills Effectiveness?		Does Application Have Potential Impact on Increasing Basic Skills Effectiveness?		Does Application Have Direct and Potential Impact for Increasing Higher-Order Skills?
	Yes	*No*	*Yes*	*No*	
Yes	CAI for certain subjects and grade levels Intelligent software	Administrative applications to reduce paperwork	Administrative applications to reduce paperwork Drill & Practice Self-service courseware		Intelligent software?
No	Simulations?	Computer-managed instruction Simulations?	Simulations?	Computer-managed instructions Simulations	Simulations? Computer programming? Networking with information utilities?
Applications That Provide "Cost Savings"	Laboratory and Driver Education Simulations				

goal (in this case, individualized instruction). As a result, CMI fails the test of appropriateness on two counts and therefore should not be considered an appropriate use of computers. A more automated CAI system is needed, one that not only can diagnose and prescribe but also can automatically provide the appropriate instruction or drill.

While CAI does have some capability to individualize the sequence of instruction, and has been shown to improve effectiveness in the area of basic skills, no software at present can really "understand" why a given student is having problems. In addition, today's CAI software can assist only in the area of basic skills. Research and development in artificial intelligence make it feasible, however, to envision software within this decade that is capable of more sophisticated diagnostic and prescriptive techniques for delivering both basic and higher-order skills. Such software will likely make it possible to increase automation of basic skill delivery (therefore increasing time savings) and will likely reduce the amount of time required to develop given levels of higher-order skills as compared to alternative conventional approaches (see Table 10 for some speculations). There is, however, virtually no research available on the automation and effectiveness potential of intelligent software—largely due to the limited amount of such software that is available or under development.

Whereas the goal of using computers in the delivery of basic skills is to automate many of the ongoing traditional interactions in classrooms, the technology-specific skills component requires providing a new set of interactions—interactions for which the automation potential is rather low for the foreseeable future. Some of the computer-specific skills include (a) computer programming, (b) word processing, (c) computer repair, (d) electronic data retrieval, (e) communications network management, and (f) electronic drafting and design. Such programs are add-ons to the curriculum and as such provide no potential for personnel time reduction or cost-savings.

There are, however, a series of computer uses that offer substantial reductions in personnel time requirements. For example, school administrators can look forward to software that will reduce time spent on paperwork, and teachers may employ programs that check compositions for spelling and grammar errors. The latter application would allow teachers more time to critique the creativity of the content. *Un-*

*der the conditions of relatively fixed personnel budgets, it becomes
essential to use computers to automate as many of the transactions in
the delivery of basic skills as possible in order to increase the potential for providing higher-order and technology use skills.*

There is, of course, some overlap between higher-order and technology-specific skills. Learning to write and debug computer programs is a highly creative process in which a student is constantly
exploring cause-and-effect relationships and engaging in problem-
solving activities. As a result, programming can be considered a se-
miautomated process for developing higher-order skills. It is therefore important to view programming from a dual perspective: that of
providing general higher-order skills and that of preparing students to
be professional programmers. Those who argue against teaching the
Basic programming language are ignoring the former function. It is
not, however, really essential to differentiate the two functions until
the tenth or eleventh grade. Prior to that period, most students can be
sequenced through a relatively similar progression of programming
activities. What is important is that this progression start at a relatively early age, since student performance and interest in math start
to drop off dramatically under conventional teaching at the early elementary grade level.

Fortunately, one of the major success stories of educational software development has been the creation of a series of children's programming languages, most of which are variations of the LOGO language developed by Seymour Papert. Papert (1980) has reported
success in teaching LOGO even to preschoolers and students labeled
as learning-disabled. Students can begin to make the transition to programming in Basic or some of the simpler authoring languages (such
as Pilot) around the fourth grade. Most microcomputers have versions
of Basic that incorporate easy-to-generate color graphics and sounds,
which young children find fascinating.

Students in the junior high and early high school years can be involved in more sophisticated programming applications in the Basic
language. It is not clear how much time students should be spending at
each of these activities and stages. Clearly, those students who have
special aptitudes and interests in the areas of programming will want to
spend more time. Such students should also have the opportunity to

learn structured languages, such as Pascal and Cobol, at the high school level. Proficiency in such languages is critical for employment as programmers and for passing the new high school advanced placement programming test. For the small percentage of students who are computer freaks, assembly language programming is also highly desirable.

A recent development is the availability of artificial intelligence systems for micros, which provide a facility for creating languages. The first such product to be marketed is SAVVY, which was developed for the Apple by Excalibur Technology. SAVVY allows an individual to teach the computer a language of his or her own creation and choice; in other words, the user can set the ground rules for person-machine communication. Although it is too early to tell what impact such a capability will have on the demand for traditional forms of programming, it does create intriguing possibilities for teaching students the nuances of regular language by having them try to teach a machine to understand their modes of communication. (Of course, such a capability may also negate the importance of uniform communication standards, such as proper English.) A capability such as SAVVY also presents the only realistic hope of adapting computer software to meet the multilingual needs of the proliferating nationalities, and their associated dialects, in the public schools. In other words, SAVVY makes it possible for one system to understand Spanish and for another to understand Italian or Vietnamese.

Differentiating the appropriateness criteria for the outcome goals of basic and higher-order skills is consistent with the most current thinking in cognitive psychology. Gagne (1982) has noted the importance of automating certain specific basic pieces of information as a prerequisite for engaging in higher-order modes of thought. Therefore, creative drill and practice software should not be dismissed as irrelevant to cognitive development. It is important to develop more intelligent types of software, but that does not negate the importance of instructional objectives related to the automation of basic skills that can be provided by nonintelligent CAI software. In addition, computerized courseware for advanced courses that are essentially informational (and that students take to complete a requirement) probably does not have to be as creative as that designed to substitute for instruction in basic courses, where it is important to stimulate the interest and curiosity that will lead to advanced study. It therefore makes more sense to construct a model that allocates different types of software to particular types of instructional objectives (as the model in this section has done) rather than engage in arguments over which kind of software is best.

This section has presented a model for assessing the appropriate role of technology in schools across a variety of instructional needs. Agreement on what schools should aspire to is not, however, sufficient. The question remains: How should they do it? The remainder of this chapter focuses on the logistics and managerial issues associated with implementing an appropriate program of instructional and administrative computer use.

4. PLANNING FOR INSTRUCTIONAL USES OF MICROCOMPUTERS

Instructional use of computers must be viewed from the context of physical program implementation. While conceptualizing what constitutes computer literacy or appropriate computer use is an interesting intellectual exercise, the resulting advice is of little utility for school district planning. General goals must be translated into specific, practicable objectives. Given constraints on money, space, personnel, and the number of students who can be serviced by a single computer, virtually no school district in this country can implement any rigorous, comprehensive program of computer use in a year. As a result, implementation of a computer use program must, because of practical considerations, be conceived of as a four-to five-year implementation process. What, then, should districts that wish to develop technologically relevant curricula do on Monday, and what is the best plan for linking instructional objectives to the acquisition of computers?

Districts typically start the process of computer acquisition by budgeting a certain amount of money for that purpose. The first questions they face are: (a) What computer should they buy? (b) What should they use them for? and (c) Where should they be placed? Aside from the lack of planning and the tendency to make acquisition decisions based on low bid, the most common mistake made by districts is to dilute the limited number of systems and place a few in each school. School-based computers are then further diluted by placing single units in a number of classrooms. This tendency to distribute available systems as widely as possible usually results from a need to minimize the political complaints that can be expected from nonrecipients. However, the opposite should occur.

Equipment should initially be concentrated in centralized clusters within targeted schools. There are three reasons for this. First, placing only one or two computers in a given classroom generates more transactions related to rationing their use than are provided in educational benefits. In other words, a few micros create more problems than help for the typical teacher. Second, economic realities militate against placing a cluster of computers in classrooms at the present time. Table 7 contains projections of economic technological opportunity in education. (Technological opportunity is defined as use of technology that costs less than $200 per student.) According to the table, it will probably not be economically feasible to place groupings of computers in the classroom until 1985. The second reason for not placing individual micros in classrooms is that such a strategy requires every

TABLE 7   Technological Opportunity for Low-Leverage Systems for Per Pupil
            Expenditures of $50-$200

Period	Technological Opportunity
1965-70	Manual programmed instruction.
1970-75	Large central computers in a district, state, or county office.
1975-80	Central minicomputers in a district office or school, used mainly for CAI and teaching programming to advanced students.
1980-85	Clusters of microcomputers in a central school location, used mainly for teaching programming to advanced students, drill and practice, and game playing; microcomputers begin to appear in the home.
1985-88	Classroom clusters of microcomputers used with courseware CAI (some intelligent capabilities), programming for increasing percentages of the school population, classroom management, etc. Central clusters of microcomputer-controlled video disk systems. Increasing numbers of microcomputers in the home.
1988-2000	Classroom clusters of microcomputers and intelligent video disk systems linked to home computers, external data bases, and other classroom clusters.

teacher to be willing, and technically competent, to undertake the responsibility of using them—an unlikely event, given the background of the typical classroom teacher. It can be anticipated, however, that as teachers become familiar with technology over time, placing computers in most of the classrooms will become increasingly feasible. Finally, allowing individual teachers or departments to obtain their own micros will create major competition among the many organizational units at the high school level. Such competition leads to uncoordinated, underutilized equipment and an environment in which systematic planning becomes almost impossible. The situation also becomes ironic in the sense that no one group has sufficient equipment to sustain a quality program or computer use experience.

Once the decision has been made to establish computer centers within schools, several other issues need to be resolved: (a) how many centers, (b) which instructional activities should be provided in each center, and (c) how many and what type of, computers should be placed in each center.

The first step in resolving these issues is to link them to a set of differentiated instructional objectives such as (a) remediation, (b) reinforcement, and (c) the development of specific computer skills. Remediation refers to using computers to help students performing substantially below grade level with CAI-type activities. Reinforcement refers to activities designed to improve higher-order skills and provide additional insights into the traditional curriculum content through simulations, drill and practice, and graphics. Specific computer skills are those needed to utilize the technology effectively; they range from programming to computer repair. While somewhat arbitrary, these three objectives have been chosen as the key categories for planning purposes because they span all the components of appropriate computer use discussed in the previous section, but differ substantially in terms of implementation requirements.

The second step in the process of developing a structure for the centers is to identify the *types of students* that will be involved with each of the objectives along with the *mode of involvement.* "Types" refers to student characteristics, such as grade and performance level, that determine how many students are available, or eligible, for a given service. For example, if a school decides to provide math CAI to all sixth-graders performing more than a year and a half below grade level, it will have to service fewer students (and need fewer computers for the remediation function) than if it decides to provide math and reading CAI to students in any grade who are performing a year below grade level. A school must determine whether certain aspects of programming will be taught to all students, whether it will offer specialized courses (such as assembly language programming), and, if so, to whom.

Once it has been determined which students will be targeted for a particular type of service, the next step is to determine the mode in which that service will be provided. The mode of involvement refers to computer utilization factors such as (a) the amount of time each targeted student will spend at the computer per day, week, or month; (b) how students will be brought to the computer center; (c) the number of students who can share a computer (pupil-computer ratio); and (d) who has responsibility for staffing the center during this activity. For example, CAI at the high school level may consist of an entire class going to the center with the teacher and an aide, with a 1:1 ratio of computers for twenty minutes for three to five days per week. CAI at the elementary level could consist of a pullout program (in which students are taken from the classroom to a lab), with the same time factors and pupil-computer ratio. Simulation activities, on the other hand, are probably best accomplished if the class as a whole goes to the center with the teacher for an hour at a time, with a 3:1 ratio.

Once the targeted students and mode of use have been identified for each instructional objective, the number of computers needed to support a given activity is calculated by the following formula:

$$\text{Number of computers} = \frac{\text{Number of students}}{\text{Mode of activity}}$$

For example, if there are 100 students targeted for CAI activities for 20 minutes 5 days a week, with a 1:1 ratio, then the number of systems needed (assuming 300 minutes available in the school day) is $100/(300/20) = 6.7$, or 7 computers. For reinforcement activities, assuming one hour per day, with a class going to the center and a 3:1 ratio, the number of systems (assuming that class size does not exceed 32 students) would be 32/3 or 11 computers.

The equipment for remediation activities typically tends to be more sophisticated and expensive ($3,500 to $5,000 per computer in 1982, compared to as little as $500 for teaching programming at the elementary level) than that required for the other objectives. As a result, it becomes very important to limit the number of students involved in the remediation function; otherwise the costs for that objective will overwhelm available resources. It is suggested that math CAI for upper elementary and high school students be given priority based on available research findings.

The *type* of computer should be determined by a committee of teachers and administrators who view available software for each of the objectives and then choose the computer for which the best software is available. The decision should be made independently for each objective—even if the process yields different computers. It is no more a problem to use multiple types of computers for different educational functions than it is to use different texts for different subjects. What is important from a managerial perspective is that the choice of each system be both systematically linked to a particular instructional objective and maintained uniformly across the district.

Table 8 contains an illustrative plan for allocating the instructional objectives across the different centers, along with recommendations for activity mode, for the elementary level. Table 9 does the same for the secondary level. Once such a framework has been established in a district planning process, it becomes possible to project the number and types of computers that will be needed, which in turn generates revenue and staffing needs. It also becomes important to project the costs for maintenance and software—costs that typically run $3,000 to $5,000 per center per year. Schools typically underinvest in software, which totally undermines the educational effort. In some cases this is done out of ignorance about the role of software. In other cases, such underinvestment results from the usually mistaken belief that the district can develop its own software.

Once costs have been projected, the next stage is to plan the phasing-in process, since it is unlikely that there will be sufficient funds or expertise to implement the plan all at once. The two primary phasing-in strategies are to establish all instructional objectives in pilot schools, phasing them in across the other schools over time, or to

TABLE 8 Sample Program for Allocating Elementary-Level Activities to Centers

Educational Objectives	CAI Center	Graphics Center	Discovery Center
Remediation	Grades 5-7 (Grades 3-4 optional) —automatic testing —automatic placement —individualized tutoring —management report for teachers —homework generation		
Reinforcement		Grades 1-7 —drill and practice with synthesizer —educational simulation and games	Grades 1-7 —drill and practice —educational simulation and games
Computer Use Skills		Grades K-4 —mathematics readiness —programming readiness —problem solving —computer art and music	Grades 5-7 —programming —word processing —computer art and music
Mode of Use	1:1 ratio Pullout, 15-20 minutes per day, 4-5 days per week, 1 system per 15-20 targeted students (depending on length of school day).	1:3 ratio (1:1 for drill and practice), whole class or half class enters 1 hour per day, 5 days per week, 1 week out of 3-5.	same
Technical Skill Requirements of Staff	None	Only for programming readiness activities	Only for programming activities.

117

implement a single objective in different schools and then expand the number of objectives in each school. It may also be desirable to establish pilot tests of the effectiveness of alternative software for a particular objective in cases where the staff is unable to reach a consensus.

The nature of the phasing-in strategy is determined partly by district-specific criteria such as perceived priority needs and available resources. In using this model, districts will typically run into the problem of inadequate resources to begin centers in each of the schools. For example, a district may have three schools, each of which may need nine computers for one center, but may be able to afford only nine computers. Should the district put three computers in each school or nine in one? The latter is the preferable strategy. By setting up a full lab in one school, the district can establish a full-scale program and evaluate the results over a period of two years. That learning process can then be the basis for establishing or not establishing similar programs when additional funds become available. If districts dilute their programs and efforts, it may take several years before any of the programs is in full gear and therefore several additional years before the district knows if there are any educational benefits from computer use. Moreover, using a targeted approach (as opposed to the one-computer-in-every-school dilution strategy) reduces the initial staff development needs while providing a model program that can help with future staff development.

External factors, such as the rate of technological development and the time needed to train personnel, also affect the phasing-in strategy. For example, low-cost high-resolution computer drafting systems will probably not be available until 1985. That suggests the point in time when districts should plan to implement that activity. If electronics instructors are expected to take a year to develop the skills needed to organize an electronics repair program, then that activity should be delayed for a year. Fortunately, relatively little training is required for most teachers to use central clusters for remediation and reinforcement activities if schools choose appropriate, highly automated software. The major training problems tend to be associated with the computer skills area, although only a minority of teachers need to be involved in that area.

As teachers become comfortable with computers as instructional

TABLE 9   Sample Program for Allocating Secondary-Level Activities to Centers

Educational Objectives	Basic Skills Center	Vocational Center	Programming Center
Remediation	Grades 8,9		
	—CAI		
	automatic testing		
	automatic placement		
	individual tutoring		
	management report for		
	teachers		
	homework generation		
	Grades 10-12		
	—proficiency practice		
Reinforcement	Grades 8-12	Grades 8-12	Grades 8-12
	—simulation	—accounting	—solving mathematics problems
		—business mathematics	via programming
		—typing	
		—electronics	
		—writing	
Computer Use Skills		Grades 8-12	Grades 8-12
		—word processing	—programming
		—network management	Basic
		—data file manipulation	Pascal
		—computer repair	Cobol
		—computer assembly	Assembly

(continued)

119

TABLE 9 (Continued)

Educational Objectives	Basic Skills	Vocational	Programming
			—graphics —drafting
Mode of use	Entire class enters	Entire class enters	Entire class enters
	CAI—1:1 ratio, 4 days per week, 15-20 minutes	1:2 ratio for entire period for at least half the semester	1:2 or 1:3 ratio used every day
	Simulation—1:3 ratio, whole period, scheduled on an as needed basis		

tools and as the cost of the technology continues to decline, it will be feasible to begin a process of phasing clusters of computers into the classroom by 1986, while establishing the next generation of expensive, intelligent video disk systems into central clusters. A process wherein newer technologies are placed in clusters (replacing the older, cheaper systems, which would be moved into classrooms) until they become more cost-effective and familiar provides a way for schools to incorporate new technologies while continuing to benefit from the older ones.

Phasing-in of technology is not, however, simply a function of changing hardware or changing modes of use. Nor is the allocation of instructional activities to particular centers by itself adequate. The fundamental key to implementing the recommended planning process for maximizing the amount of appropriate computer use activities provided to students is to limit or focus the types of automated interactions that are provided to those which research can show to meet one of the three criteria of appropriateness. In particular, it is important to limit the types of instructional interactions (in the reinforcement and remediation categories) provided by technology to those that offer a relative advantage (in terms of time, effectiveness, or cost) over attempting to provide such services via traditional teaching. Over time, as technological opportunity and the quality of research increase, it can be expected that the number of instructional interactions for which technology offers an appropriate advantage will also increase.

While it is impossible to predict what research will find with respect to specific applications and new forms of technology, Table 10 contains some speculations on how the relative advantage of technology will shift over time. It must be emphasized that these speculations are undocumented and are included only for the purpose of illustrating the implications of the likelihood that the relative advantage will start to shift toward technology for increasing numbers of applications as the decade progresses.

It is the focusing of the computer use effort in centers and classrooms on those that meet the criteria of appropriateness (at a given point in time) that makes it possible for districts to maximize the educational benefits received for their investment in technology. Such focusing is also the key to using technology as a low-leverage delivery system.

TABLE 10 Potential Relative Advantage of Teacher Versus Technology under Present and Future Conditions of Technological Opportunity

Time Frame	Human	Technology
1983-87	—Reading drill and practice —Virtually all teaching —Ethics/philosophy/poetry —Grading essays	—Math drill and practice —Math and reading readiness (?) —Mathematical (symbolic) thinking —Scientific discovery process thinking readiness (?) —Information access and aggregation —Music theory (?) —Correcting spelling —Grading multiple-choice exams —Problem-solving skills —Paperwork management
1987 on	—Most teaching	—Math drill, practice math, and reading readiness —Mathematical (symbolic) thinking —Scientific discovery process thinking readiness —Information access and aggregation —Music theory (?) —Correcting spelling —Grading multiple-choice exams —Problem-solving skills —Paperwork management —Diagnosing learning problems —Diagnosing reasons for student errors in math —Diagnosing reasons for student errors in reading (?) —Delivering highly specialized courses in math and science —Correcting grammar —Interactive courseware on demand in the home and school (10-15 years)

Although it is important for districts to engage in the recommended planning process, that does not mean that they should adopt the specific plan contained in Tables 8 and 9. There is no rule that there must be three, instead of two or four, central clusters; that the equipment in two of the clusters should not be periodically combined for use at the same time by a single class; that there cannot be more than one type of computer in each cluster; or that each district must provide all three instructional objectives. What is important is that these decisions should be made as part of a conscious, highly participative process in which the computer is viewed as a curricular device rather than a piece of capital equipment, and in which there is a conscious effort by the participants to identify the best software for a predefined, specific, appropriate instructional objective.

5. PLANNING FOR ADMINISTRATIVE USES OF COMPUTERS

According to Table 4, appropriate administrative uses of computers are those that provide substantial savings in personnel time required to accomplish paperwork tasks. Such time reductions provide the potential for enhancing basic skills effectiveness if teachers use the freed-up time to increase time on instructional tasks, and administrators, to increase instructional supervision time. Unfortunately, districts are replete with examples of inappropriate administrative computer use, i.e., uses that, rather than produce time savings, actually increase the trauma and time associated with paperwork. This section will discuss how to implement a cost-effective program of administrative use of microcomputers. The focus will be on microcomputers because they are what most districts can afford and will be using.

Inappropriate administrative uses of computers result largely from administrators' reluctance to evaluate software carefully. Districts considering a software program seldom do more than a cursory evaluation of the product they are considering, and such evaluation tends to focus on the types of reports generated. While it is important that the program generate the kind of reports an administrator needs, a program can produce the needed reports and still result in a net increase in the amount of paperwork that must be handled. Net paperwork reduction requires an intensive evaluation not only of what comes out of the computer, but also what goes in and how it goes in and is changed.

The nonautomated aspects of computer use involve assembling, entering, and modifying the system data. If a computer system is to produce a net time-saving, *the time required to assemble the data for computer entry, plus the time to enter the data and make necessary modifications to the computerized data, must be less than the amount of time required to assemble the data and calculate the results manually*. This requirement will be met if the following conditions exist:

(a) The computer program must perform extensive processing operations on each piece of data entered into the system.

(b) The number of subsequent changes that need to be made because of errors at the time of data entry must be minimal, because each piece of data that must be corrected has the net effect of at least tripling the labor involved in entering information. (This assumes that it takes time to determine that an error has been made, as well as why or where.)

(c) Those responsible for assembling the data should also be able to enter the data directly into the computer, and those responsible for using the data should be able to retrieve specific pieces of information directly and on their own (with close to immediate system response).

(d) When changes need to be made in the data or report formats because of changing circumstances, they must be able to be made directly (preferably immediately) on the computer by those either assembling or responsible for using the data.

These conditions will hereafter be referred to as the *basic principles for automating paperwork*.

The seemingly obvious first principle is widely violated—usually because of a failure to work by exception or the tendency to computerize applications with relatively trivial processing requirements. Working by exception means that only those components of an application that cause the greatest problems, and hence have a clear time-saving potential, should be computerized. For example, suppose you wanted to use the computer to track student immunization status and set up a system for that specific purpose. Since only a relatively small percentage of students tend not to be in compliance shortly after the start of the school year, it is a waste of time to enter all the students into the system. Rather, it makes more sense to wait a few days, and then enter only those students who are not in compliance and who therefore will require extensive amounts of monitoring and processing. While it is not always feasible to work by exception, there are substantial numbers of applications in schools where only 20 percent of the students, or transactions, generate 80 percent of the paperwork.

The other violation of the first principle is caused by the tendency of districts to exert tremendous manual effort to enter data into a system that does relatively little processing. One example would be where student course requests are laboriously entered into a computer only to produce the tally and conflict matrices. (The tally matrix is a report showing the total number of student requests for each course. This is used to help estimate the number of sections that will be needed. The conflict matrix shows the number of times that students who have requested course A have also requested course B, for all possible combinations. High levels of conflicts indicate that sections of the given courses should be scheduled for different periods.) These matrices provide data that help develop the school's master schedule; unfortunately, they cannot assist in the far more time-consuming task of student scheduling. The latter operation would still have to be done by hand. What would obviously be more desirable is if the computer could use the same manually inputed course-request data to schedule the students once the master schedule has been developed. Even more desirable would be if the computer-derived schedules automatically generated class lists for keeping attendance and also produced a computer file for entering grades. Better still would be an additional capability to enter classes automatically into a transcript file that is available to counselors. In other words, a comprehensive student scheduling program should allow the same data entry process to generate at least five interrelated tasks instead of one.

Another example of limited-utility programs are period-by-period attendance systems that produce lists of absent students but require teachers to apply those lists to determine for themselves who is cutting. With additional processing capabilities, the program could easily be designed to check for cutters on its own, producing lists of guilty students—a step that would save teachers substantial amounts of time. Unfortunately, most currently available microcomputer programs for administrative applications perform only limited, highly specific processes, despite their seductive promotional literature.

These should be avoided by administrators in favor of the more expensive but more highly integrated programs.

The second principle of paperwork automation refers to the tendency of software developers to skimp on routines for trapping errors (a very important aspect of processing). If one makes a data entry mistake at most points in most programs, one of two things usually happens. Either the program accepts the erroneous data or the system becomes confused and freezes or crashes. In the first case you now have bad data in the system; in the second you have to restart the program with a good chance that most of the data previously entered on that shift have been lost. In either case, extensive additional work is required for debugging and data entry, which are the most labor-intensive of the computer-related operations. It is not unusual for an administrator to have to spend half a day tracking down the cause of, and correcting, a single error. Many administrators, faced with the nightmare of rectifying printout errors while under time pressures, tend to wonder whether they were better off before they computerized. In such cases, they probably were.

It should be the responsibility of the computer program to automate the editing process at the time of data entry. This involves automatically performing a number of checks on each piece of data entered into the system for format accuracy and reasonableness. When an error is found, the program should provide some feedback on the nature of the error rather than simply blink its cursor at you. While the program cannot anticipate all possible types of entry errors, it certainly should not allow a clerk to enter a student into a course that does not exist. In addition, the program should provide some related data to provide visual feedback to help the individual check the entry. For example, if a clerk enters a course number, the system should respond with the name of the class, the teacher, and the time of day, so that it becomes easier for the individual to determine immediately whether a wrong number was entered and to make a change if necessary. Every error caught at the time of data entry saves far more extensive labor later on.

The third and fourth principles of paperwork automation are designed to eliminate the multiple manual steps between the stages of

(a) data assembly and entry, (b) discovery of the need to make a change and doing it, and (c) the identification of the need for data and their availability. It is important to eliminate as many of the intermediary, paper-shuffling steps between each of these processes as possible (short of compromising financial security), because they all take time, a commodity we are trying to save.

In order to understand the concept of eliminating intermediate steps, consider the following two approaches to computerizing the process of recording attendance. In the first approach, each teacher sends down the punched cards for each absent student; these are run through the computer, which produces a list of absentees. The cards, however, then have to be reassembled for delivery back to the teacher; the warped ones have to be taken out of the pile and repunched; and new students must have their information coded upon entry into the school. This information is then sent to the keypuncher. All of these steps take a lot of time, and most could be eliminated by simply having teachers send the names of absent students on paper scraps and keying these data directly into the computer.

Making changes in stored data is often fraught with time-consuming intermediate steps. A case in point is the school scheduling process. Computer programs typically produce student schedules for the entire student body in the late spring for the coming school year. By the time school is ready, some students have left, new students have been registered, others have unexpectedly failed courses which they must retake, and everyone wants to change assigned classes. This is usually handled by having the counselors develop schedules by hand and then send the information to clerks in triplicate, who enter the data into the computer and send confirmations to the teacher, dean, and back to the counselor. A simpler approach would be for the counselor to enter the needed courses into the computer, letting the computer schedule the changes and new students and produce the documents needed for the student, teacher, and dean. Since as many as 20 to 40 percent of the programs may have to be changed, the time-savings from eliminating the manual intermediate steps can be extensive.

Making changes is particularly troublesome in punched card systems (or other forms of batch processing systems) wherein data cannot be keyed directly into the computer. In batch systems, a wide variety of source documents must be prepared and shifted from person to person until the information can be entered into the system. In many applications, the time lapse between assembling the data for the change and entering them into the system can be days or weeks.

One of the most time-consuming interactions with computers is the process of retrieving data. Administrators typically get only occasional printouts from the central computer system. To make matters worse, these printouts are usually already out of date when they arrive. Special requests for data normally require the administrator to cajole some computer technician to interrupt his or her routine in order to extract the needed information from the system. The coping strategy that most administrators adopt is to maintain parallel manual systems on which they rely for current information. The central computer system thus provides little net reduction in the time required to perform administrative tasks.

When administrators need an answer to a question, information has value only if it is accurate and easily and (relatively) immediately obtainable. This is as true for paper record systems as for computer files. Thus, the only way a computer system can save time is if needed information can be easily and quickly extracted, and the only cost-effective way to do this (as opposed to providing each administrator with a technical staff) is for administrators to retrieve the needed information from the computer on their own. The minute that administrators have to delegate this responsibility, with all the communication problems inherent in conveying needs through a series of intermediary steps, there is little likelihood of a net time gain over simply doing the process manually from the start.

Both the third and fourth principles of appropriate characteristics of administrative software imply the use of software with which administrators and their nontechnical staff can easily interact and on which they can perform operations traditionally reserved for programmers. Are such expectations feasible? Computer systems have undergone substantial evolution over the past half decade and are increasingly designed with ease of use as a key feature. Will administrators take advantage of simple-to-use advanced features to interact directly with computers? Keen (1979) has demonstrated that administrators in corporations will indeed take advantage of the opportunity to design their own systems and data retrieval activities. Is such an approach feasible for education, and how could it be implemented within a limited budget for software acquisition? The answer to these questions is yes if administrators are willing to curb their natural inclination to seek specific solutions to all specific problems.

The key to implementing a strategy wherein administrators self-automate system design and data acquisition/modification activities is to apply general computer programs whenever possible to the solution of specific problems. This is because most administrative applications in education have no specific algorithmic requirements; instead, they are combinations of a variety of general procedures that are common to most administrative applications. Different applications are then different combinations of these general elements. Rather than describing the individual elements in detail, it is easier to describe the various types of general administrative software that are available and the types of functions for which they can be used.

There are three basic categories of general programs. The first is word processing programs, which provide the capability for creating and, more important, editing electronic text. When combined with capabilities for mailing labels and variable insertion into standardized forms, word processing programs provide substantial time-savings for a wide variety of document preparation and customized mailing applications, at both the school and district offices. The potential applications range from producing interoffice memos, curriculum guides, and contracts to conducting mass or selective mailings to parents, vendors, and the like.

The second type of general administrative program is the electronic spreadsheet. The original program of this type was Visicalc, but there are now upwards of forty different programs on the market. Electronic spreadsheet programs provide the capability to tabulate the results from a series of interconnected calculations on the cells of a table of data, and to examine quickly the implications of changes in the values of one or more of the variables (cells) on the final result. This can be used to assist administrators in any application in which a table of largely numerical information is involved. This includes attendance, budget control, financial planning, and student projections. Electronic spreadsheet programs can even be used for curriculum mapping applications in which it is necessary to keep track of the amount of instructional time allocated across a range of objectives.

The ability of spreadsheet programs to examine the implications of simulated changes in the data on the overall results of the systems makes it ideal for use in salary negotiations. It is rather simple to construct a spreadsheet model that can determine the fiscal implications of changes in the proposed salary or benefits schedule in seconds. Such estimates normally take days to calculate manually, and a specific salary negotiations program could cost as much as $10,000. New versions of spreadsheet programs, more powerful yet simpler to use, continue to be developed.

The third kind of general program is the data base management system (DBMS). These programs provide electronic filing capabilities. Almost all record-keeping applications can be automated with a DBMS. In addition, most such programs contain report generators so that it is relatively easy to define and redefine the structure of reports. It is even possible to reconstruct the data base to add variables without losing the data already stored. The potential applications are myriad and include maintaining student records, inventory records, vendor files, records of purchase orders, personnel records, substitute teacher files, and student discipline and medical referrals.

There are four major advantages to using such software as opposed to relying on specific-application programs. First of all, general programs are inexpensive, ranging in cost from $100 to $700, and are cost-effective in that a single program can be used for many different applications. The second advantage is that they are relatively bug-free in that they are sold to a much larger market than just educators. As a result, vendors have greater incentives to make such software as state-of-the-art and as reliable as possible. The third advantage is that they are so widely used outside education that they are available at most local neighborhood computer stores, along with training and assistance. The final, and most significant, advantage is that because they are so simple to use, most application needs can be directly implemented on these systems by the administrators themselves, even if they have no prior computer experience. It takes only two days to train reasonably intelligent administrators to set up their own system using a DBMS.

It is therefore feasible to envision administrators using general administrative software on micros to establish automated record-keeping systems in schools without the addition of technical staff. Pogrow (1982a) recommends general software programs available in 1982 that are best suited to easily establishing the types of automated management systems needed in education. These systems can even be used in large districts that already have large computer systems for easy automation of the many subsystem needs that arise. Subsystem needs are applications that apply only to a subset of the school population and for which the central data processing staff may be reluctant to develop systems. Examples include keeping track of special student populations or students who do not meet immunization standards.

While general software can automate a substantial portion of a school's paperwork burden, the major limitation of these programs is that they cannot help with the highly algorithmic processes of student scheduling and financial accounting. These latter applications require specific-application software. The traditional options for obtaining such programs have been to use computer service bureaus or, in the case of larger districts, to purchase software for use on the district's own large computers or to hire in-house programmers to develop their own software. The problem for most districts is that the services obtained are often inflexible and slow, while minicomputer software for these applications can cost upwards of $80,000. In-house software development projects are also very expensive and often/usually fail to produce quality programs.

A new alternative for these applications is to purchase software programs that are designed to function on microcomputers. A number of companies are now providing such software. While many of the available programs are of poor quality, a number of these companies appear committed to providing high-quality software for these applications at a cost of $5,000 to $10,000. Pogrow (1982b, 1982c) surveys available systems.

It is therefore feasible for administrators to use low-cost microcomputers to reduce their paperwork substantially. Such an outcome requires a strategy of using general software to automate most administrative applications and using specific programs only in the limited instances in which general software cannot be easily applied. The concept of administrators and staffs using computers as personal workstations is technically and fiscally feasible. What is critical, however, is that administrators get personally involved in evaluating whatever software they may be considering to see if it is consistent with the principles for automating paperwork.

6. FINANCING HARDWARE AND SOFTWARE ACQUISITION AT THE LOCAL LEVEL

Cost estimates performed for school districts by this author in 1982 revealed that implementation of the instructional program suggested in this chapter tends to run at 1 to 2 percent of operating expense at the high school level (excluding the cost of additional aides or reconstruction of facilities). More than half this cost is for the remediation function; thus, in schools without significant remediation needs, the figure would be .5 to 1 percent of operating expenses. This assumes an ongoing commitment rather than a one-shot expenditure, so that districts can continue to incorporate new technology. The cost at the elementary level tends to run about 1 to 4 percent of current operating costs, depending on the size of the school (this does not include the cost of aides, reconstruction, or a traveling resource teacher). To a large extent, the cost of extra aides can be eliminated by redeploying existing ones or, in the typical case where schools are being forced to riff their remaining aides, to substitute parent volunteers and student assistants. In 1982, administrative stations (including hardware and software) cost between $2,500 and $12,000 apiece, depending on their function.

One can argue over the prohibitiveness of such costs. Clearly, such a plan would not be feasible if the estimated costs were to be on the order of 20 percent or more of the existing budget. Even 2 to 4 percent of operating costs represents a large amount of dollars in absolute terms, particularly at a time when budgets are already constrained. While it is seductively simple to say that it is therefore necessary to have a new federal or state categorical funding program to enable districts to acquire hardware and software, such is not necessarily the case. First of all, expenses in the range of 2 percent of the budget can be funded largely through budgetary tradeoffs. For example, increasing pupil-teacher ratios by three students or constraining salary increases that would otherwise be forthcoming by 3 percent for one year, would free up the necessary funds.

Although teacher unions will not support these strategies for financing the acquisition of technology, educators must realize that they are facing the same situation threatening the automobile, steel, and almost every other major industry in this country: the need to build a modern technological base under conditions of declining revenue and credit ratings. There is only one way to do this: by extracting some (temporary) labor concessions.

Under conditions wherein most large organizations are being forced to extract labor concessions, the failure of educators to do so will not be greeted with much public sympathy. Rather than directly forcing the issue politically, administrators can use a strategy that will be referred to as *creative pessimism*. Under creative pessimism, one assumes the future will be slightly worse than the present, but that, rather than waiting for the future, one slightly worsens the present in order to free up some funds. For example, if you suspect that your aides or secretaries will be reduced next year, budget for fewer this year and use the savings to put a technological alternative in place in case your fears are realized. Another approach would be simply not to replace individuals who leave in the middle of the year in order to free up funds for technology. It might be difficult, however, to apply such savings in the operations portion of the budget to purchasing computers or software under the accounting restrictions that currently exist in most states (recommendations for revising such systems are included in Chapter VII).

Less controversial options are available to districts. Schools interested in developing an intensive technology program are finding ways to link this goal with a variety of traditional funding sources and are also using entrepreneurism to create new ones. Examples of the former include (a) the use of adult education funds to establish centers that are used by the schools during the day, (b) vocational education funds, and (c) the new federal block grant program. Examples of entrepreneurial behavior include (a) renting out computers to parents or small businesses over the weekends and holidays, (b) setting up game arcades (preferably instructional ones) in the computer centers for student use, at a nominal cost during lunch, (c) PTA fund-raising activities, and (d) selling buildings and properties no longer needed because of declining enrollment. Districts can generate substantial revenues to support technology through these and other creative financing schemes.

It appears, therefore, that if the will and creativity are there, districts can fund substantial portions of hardware and software even within existing budgetary constraints. At the same time, districts do differ in demographic characteristics, which can affect the feasibility of generating revenue by means of the foregoing ideas. Alleviating the effects that such noncontrollable systematic variations in self-revenue generate for technology acquisition will be viewed as a primary policy issue.

7. POLICY AND RESEARCH IMPLICATIONS

This chapter has described what constitutes a technologically relevant curriculum and appropriate instructional uses of computers in education. The question obviously remains as to whether or not schools will adapt in a substantive way to the demands of the new technology by the 1985-87 period. Chapter IV discussed the many constraints that can inhibit or prevent such adaptation. As promised, this work will not attempt to speculate on whether schools will in fact overcome these constraints. Rather, and more important, this work differentiates between constraints that are self-imposed (i.e., derive from the unwillingness of educators to change traditional norms) and those that are externally imposed, in order to suggest policies that can alleviate the effects of the latter. The general policy goal is to create an environment wherein those schools that want to achieve technological relevance, and are willing to make "reasonable" sacrifices to achieve such a goal, will be able to do so.

The basic goal of policy will be viewed as providing equal opportunity for districts desiring to use technology appropriately to be able to do so on an ongoing basis. The "ongoing" component of the definition is important, because as technology changes, activities that are not now educationally feasible or appropriate will become so. That does not mean that one should wait for the next millennium (and there will probably always be a next one) to begin to use technology; rather, one should take appropriate educational advantage of the present generation of technology while preparing to employ the new capabilities as they become available. As a result, the policy recommendations in the next two chapters have a dual focus. The first is on removing external constraints related to the appropriate use of existing technological capabilities; the second concerns reducing the effects of anticipatable future constraints on the use of the next generation of technology (e.g., intelligent video disk and intelligent software).

This, of course, brings us back to the question that began this chapter: How can one determine what is appropriate use of technology? In Table 6, which outlines the general model for determining appropriate uses of computers, many of the cell entries contain question marks. Although existing research provides sufficient guidance for making a number of key utilization decisions, there is a great deal of uncertainty surrounding others. For example, do simulations and programming experience contribute to higher-order skill development, and if so, how much time on task is required to achieve such outcomes? What is the extent of expected automation potential for training teachers to use technology to deliver a variety of key skills rather than having them deliver the skills by themselves? What is the best mode of use, particularly in terms of amount of time allocated, for applying technology to reinforce curricular objectives?

The next two chapters discuss the policy and research agenda that is needed to support the model that has been suggested for implementing low-leverage delivery systems in schools. Considering policies to enable "appropriate" use of computers to begin prior to completion of the research agenda to fully define the parameters of such use may seem inappropriate. It is essential, however, to begin to pursue policies to minimize the effects of the constraints, since the ones that may interfere with applications that future research finds to be appropriate are the same ones that will inhibit those applications (in the model in Table 6) which are already known to be appropriate. It is therefore important to address key policy issues immediately, while a research effort is under way to validate or reject the other components in the model.

VI FEDERAL POLICY AND RESEARCH ISSUES

      IF SCHOOLS ARE to adapt and use technology in appropriate ways, it is necessary to overcome existing barriers to such use. The structural barriers (as discussed in Chapter IV) basically cluster into the following categories: (a) personnel shortages, (b) shortages of quality software, (c) funding limitations, and (d) political resistance. In addition, operationalizing the definition of "appropriate" uses of technology (as discussed in Chapter V) requires more detailed knowledge of the cost-effectiveness of a greater variety of potential computer uses than is currently available. Since developing more technologically relevant schools is critical for our national economy and may also be essential for our national defense, overcoming these barriers can be considered (at least partially) a federal policy issue. It remains to be determined, however, what the federal role and responsibility should be vis-à-vis the other levels of government. In addition, it remains to be determined which specific federal interventions would be appropriate and feasible under conditions of constrained resources.

Clearly, it makes little sense for the federal government to try to ameliorate the effects of all of the barriers or to try to solve single-handedly all the problems associated with any of them. For example, it makes little sense for the federal government to deal with the issue of expected political resistance. It is also not clear what the government could or should do about shortages of technical personnel, which are largely caused by market and free enterprise factors. On the other hand, the federal government does have greater expertise in organizing research and development programs, a wider revenue base, and a broader philosophical perspective on equity issues than do other levels of government. As a result, the federal role will be conceived as contributing needed R & D efforts, as well as funding, for those aspects of need that would or could not otherwise be addressed or funded at the local or state level. In addition, it appears that the particular barriers that can be most affected by these unique contributions are inadequate knowledge bases and software shortages.

This chapter will therefore explore how the federal government can use its R & D-generation and unique funding capabilities to provide the knowledge and the forms and quantities of software that are critical if schools are to develop more technologically relevant curricula. Before specific proposals are explored, however, we must deal with the issue of whether it is necessary for the federal government to get involved rather than follow a laissez-faire policy.

1. LIMITS OF ENVIRONMENTAL COLLAPSE

Although the technology relevance of schools is an issue of national concern, if the free market mechanism of environmental collapse can ensure adequate alternatives to the public school system, there is no need for federal intervention. There are, however, three problems with relying solely on environmental collapse to solve the problem of technology relevance. First, there is no guarantee that environmental collapse will occur rapidly or comprehensively enough to meet most educational needs or provide enough skilled workers. The second problem is that the generation of many small private institutions could increase social fragmentation and segregation. The final limitation of a dependence on environmental collapse is that access to training in technology could become a function of wealth. If such training were available only in private schools or public schools in wealthy areas, the poor would be at a gross disadvantage when competing for jobs in a changing economy. This could lead to a situation Licklider (1979) has referred to as the "electronic ghetto" and could introduce disparities in opportunity that are far more damaging than those addressed by school finance in the seventies.

These limitations, however, do not mean that the federal government should make the prevention of environmental collapse its primary policy focus. Aside from the constitutional and philosophical objections to such a policy goal, the lesson of the past decade is that it is difficult for the federal government to stimulate the widespread adoption and implementation of innovation among resistant institutions. As a result, if public schools are not predisposed to reorient their curriculum, environmental collapse is likely to be more effective than federal policy in providing incentives for the public schools to change or ensuring that appropriate alternatives exist if they do not.

A noninterventionist federal policy perspective that relies on environmental collapse is, therefore, not adequate for dealing with the problem of technological relevance. At the same time, federal policy initiatives that focus on preventing environmental collapse or that simply continue to focus on the equity issues of the seventies (improving effectiveness and distributional equity) are inadequate. What does seem appropriate, however, are interventionist policies that retain the kernel of existing broad federal concern for promoting equity but also focus on the equity concerns that are particular to an era of changing technology and constrained resources.

2. EQUITY ISSUES AND FEDERAL POLICY

Two major equity issues are likely to result from the impact and potential of changing technology during this decade. The first is *access equity*. Access equity is the distribution of opportunity to acquire the skills necessary to compete for jobs in the 1990 high-technology world of work, and the extent to which the distribution is a function of wealth. Access equity can also include disparities in the distribution of home learning opportunities due to the inability of the poor to purchase home computers or cable hookups.

The second technology equity issue is *efficiency equity:* the extent to which the maximum amount of needed educational activities that can be provided with available resources are in fact made available. In other words, if there is a potential for increasing the amount of services provided per unit cost by integrating appropriate uses of technology into the instructional process, under conditions where an absolute increase in instructional services is likely to improve student learning outcomes and/or opportunity, there is probably some point at which the rights of students supersede the potential desire of institutions to maintain the status quo. Whether there are legal precedents for supporting this contention or forming a class action suit is beyond the scope of this work. If, however, the use of technology is the only way to increase the amount of educational services that can be provided, it does seem appropriate from an egalitarian equity perspective to develop federal policies that promote the availability and use of such technology.

Achieving high levels of either access equity or efficiency equity requires the widespread availability of technology. The greater the degree of availability, the less likely it is that a particular group will control access to it. Technology availability is, however, a function of (a) technological opportunity, which determines whether existing technology can provide needed capabilities, and (b) market forces, which determine whether such capability will be commercially available. A minimum federal role would be to intervene where market forces are not providing technology that is necessary for efficiency equity but for which technological opportunity exists. In other words, the federal role can initially be viewed as narrowing the gap between technological opportunity and technological availability.

Widespread availability of technology, however, while minimizing the risk that one group will be at an unfair advantage with regard to access, does not guarantee that inequities will not occur. This suggests a two-pronged federal approach. The first would be devoted to eliminating gaps between technological opportunity and availability by stimulating (if necessary) widespread availability. Since technological opportunity will exist for large-scale sophisticated use in education by the 1985-87 period, federal policy should initially focus on removing market impediments prior to that point in time. The second prong of federal involvement should be a research agenda to measure access equity and to develop policies to alleviate disparities of wealth-related access equity, should they appear.

3. THE FEDERAL ROLE IN ELIMINATING MARKET IMPEDIMENTS

To date legislative initiatives that have proposed a role for federal involvement in educational technology have focused on providing assistance for the purchase of hardware. However, since there is a sufficiently large market for hardware outside education for its cost to continue to decline rapidly, it can be expected that the market availability of hardware will match technological opportunity without additional federal policy intervention, such as subsidies for the acquisition of hardware by school districts. (There may, however, be a different rationale for federal hardware subsidies, as will be discussed later in this chapter.) Apple, IBM, and the other computer vendors are doing fine without government subsidies.

The major market impediment to technological availability in education involves the development of appropriate kinds of software. The basic view in Washington at present is that *all* software development is a responsibility of the private sector or the states. Such a view is simplistic and potentially harmful. Although it is true that the private sector is undertaking a role in educational software development, and it is important and necessary that states get involved in stimulating the educational software market (suggestions for which are contained in Chapter VII), such involvement will not remove all the barriers to software availability. Software development policy must recognize that there are different kinds of software and different barriers for particular types of software. In addition, removing some of the barriers requires special R & D activities that are best carried out at the federal level. Identifying which kinds of software intervention policies are needed at the federal level is the focus of the remainder of this section.

As already noted, the market is likely to provide the necessary software for basic drill and practice. One major software need and technological opportunity by mid-decade will be intelligent instructional software. However, even though the hardware for such software currently exists, it is unlikely that publishing companies will invest the sums needed to produce the software necessary to support more advanced types of cognitive development before mid-decade, given the current small market and inadequate safeguards against piracy (which further limits the size of the market). Whereas advanced types of hardware will continue to be developed because they can be sold to large business and government markets, educational software has only a limited, and as yet unreliable, education market.

Advances in artificial intelligence and learning theory have clearly created the technological potential to develop software that can provide higher-order skill interactions as well as diagnose and remediate learning problems. Such software would permit more extensive forms of technological substitution to occur and would create the potential for major increases in efficiency and cost reductions. It would also allow instruction in technical areas where the worst of the teacher shortages now exist and would facilitate self-learning in areas, particularly higher-order skill activities in math and science, that are generally poorly taught.

The only way such software will be produced during this decade, however, is if the federal government underwrites the basic research and development costs. The goal of such a program would be to conduct research on the best way to structure such software for a variety of key subject areas, and then develop and test a series of prototypes. It would also be important to develop a series of programming aids to facilitate the development of such systems. Such a program would probably require a relatively modest commitment of $20 to $30 million per year for five years.

Because the educational software market is small, there is a shortage of high-quality conventional software. As previously noted, at this point the large publishing houses are hedging their bets, producing highly conventional computer materials that basically emulate their books. There is little attempt to incorporate the unique capabilities of the computer or existing knowledge about the learning process into the design of instructional software. For example, few of the results from NIE research on reading have been incorporated into existing software products. In addition, while a number of federal agencies, such as the Department of Defense and the National Science Foundation, are funding research on artificial intelligence that has implications for the design of instructional software, there has been little formal linkage between these fields.

There are several ways the federal government could remove impediments to the production of high-quality conventional (as opposed to intelligent) software. The government could encourage expansion of the educational software market by providing subsidies for schools to purchase software or tax incentives for individuals or organizations to make software donations. Unfortunately, there is no guarantee that such a policy would stimulate vendors to improve the quality of their products or to develop more advanced types of software. Given the relative lack of sophistication among school practitioners at present, with respect to evaluating instructional software, it would be far easier for vendors to concentrate on marketing their existing products. As sophistication on the part of practitioners increases, however, their growing selectivity within an expanding market could begin to force vendors to develop more sophisticated software. As school district expenditures for software increase in 1983 (as compared to 1982), the number of new, highly creative educational software products that are also being introduced in 1983 are increasing (again, as compared to 1982), although the vast majority of such programs are produced by small companies. Whether the external stimulation of the growth of the software market will continue to lead to the production of more examples of creative conventional software applications remains to be seen. Nor is it clear why such market stimulation should be a federal rather than a state responsibility. However, if the federal government were to initiate a special program to stimulate the use of computers in schools, the funding of software acquisition should be a higher priority than software.

An alternative, relatively low-cost, approach to stimulating production of quality conventional educational software would be for the government to reduce the cost of market entry. Much of the quality software in the business sector has been developed by individuals or small groups rather than large organizations. The low capital costs associated with producing software have spawned an extensive "garage industry" of developers. Discussion about the state of educational software always seems to center on what the large publishers are doing. There is an enormous potential for a garage industry in educational software that would expand the quantity and quality of available products.

There is, however, a major impediment to the development of a garage industry for the production of educational software. While the capital costs of developing software are low, the marketing costs are high. In the private sector, good software can attract venture capital to subsidize the marketing effort. Alternatively, the business sector is so large that companies can make a large profit just from marketing on a local regional basis and then use those profits to market nationally.

The marketing costs for educational software are as high as for commercial software, but the market is so much smaller that it is virtually impossible for a low-capital operation to compete in the market. As of right now, entrepreneurs who develop software programs for education have only one real option if they want to make money, and that is to license their programs to large publishing or supplies distribution companies. Unfortunately, this gives a few companies a near-monopoly on determining what will be available to schools and these companies often are seeking to maximize the return on their existing product line. Of course, in some areas of the country local markets are sufficiently large that a profit can be made by entrepreneurs through regional marketing alone. One can find examples of excellent educational software available on a regional basis in places such as California and New York but largely unavailable (with training and service) in other parts of the country.

It appears, therefore, that a garage industry producing educational software could result in major increases in the quantity, availability, and quality of materials. Since the goal would be to stimulate such availability on a national basis, federal intervention would be appropriate. The best and cheapest way for the federal government to stimulate the development of a garage industry for producing educational software would be to subsidize the marketing costs for selected software products for a period of one to two years. If the product were successful, the sales from the initial period would sustain future marketing efforts and software development for that company. Assuming that it takes $30,000 to $50,000 per year (including travel, partial salary of sales personnel, and advertising) to market a software product or series of products, it would be possible to support the distribution of twenty to thirty major software products a year for $1 million.

In addition to low cost, such an entrepreneurial support program has the advantage of enabling the government to influence the areas in which new software development occurs. For example, in setting criteria for selecting the software products to be supported, the government could indicate that priority would be given to a complete science course, a program to teach language arts to non-English-speaking children, and so on.

While a proposal such as the entrepreneurial support program may seem nontraditional, there is actually precedence for such a federal program in the National Science Foundation's small-business technology development program. The goal of this program is to assist small businesses that have developed promising technologies in marketing the ideas to venture capitalists. If the design of the new technology is promising, NSF will provide support to the company to develop and demonstrate prototypes, thereby giving the company a chance to attract the financial support it needs to bring the product to market.

Although the large companies might oppose such an entrepreneurial support program, the program could be supplemented with an equal expenditure to subsidize the development of high-quality software in publishing companies in priority subject areas. Priority areas and standards for such programs would depend on the following factors:

(a) anticipated technological opportunity based on research findings, theory, and new technological capabilities (see Tables 7 and 10 for some speculations);
(b) the extent to which student performance is declining in a particular skill area;
(c) time- and cost-savings that would be generated by the use of a certain type of software; and

(d) the extent to which there are critical personnel shortages in a particular subject area.

While the proposed software development programs will not solve the problems of personnel shortages or the declining quality of the teaching work force, they offer one way to ameliorate the effects of these problems until better solutions can be found.

The policies suggested in this section are designed to help remove barriers to the generation of adequate types and amounts of instructional software by creating the necessary R & D base and expanding the market and supply. The combination of policies is intended to maintain congruence between the technological opportunities that are becoming available as a result of evolving hardware, and the availability of software that fulfills the educational potential of the new equipment. The first part of the program will make it possible for a variety of intelligent software to be available in about five years, to interface with a new generation of cost-effective micros with advanced graphic capabilities and intelligent video disk systems. This will ensure wide availability of intelligent instructional technology at the point when public demand and the economic necessity for such technology are expected to increase rapidly. The entrepreneurial support programs are designed to fill the conventional software gap over the short term, using essentially existing low-cost technology.

The combination of software development approaches that have been recommended will have the net effect of maximizing the amount of technological substitution that is feasible under low-leverage delivery systems. There still remains, however, the research problem of determining which forms of technological substitutions are appropriate. There is a chicken-and-egg problem in that appropriateness (or lack thereof) of substituting technology for a particular aspect of instruction cannot be determined in the absence of quality software prototypes. In addition, once the appropriateness of substituting technology for a particular instructional task has been determined, there is the question of how access to the technological form of the instruction can be distributed equitably. The next section deals with the research implications of generating the knowledge bases needed to answer these questions.

4. RESEARCH IMPLICATIONS OF EFFICIENCY EQUITY

Efficiency equity refers to the extent to which technological substitution occurs for tasks for which such substitution is appropriate (based on the three appropriateness criteria—time-saving, effectiveness improvement, and cost-saving), thereby making it possible to increase the quantity and quality of educational services that are provided per unit cost. The key research issue in measuring efficiency equity is determining the particular instructional tasks for which substitution is appropriate under different conditions of technological opportunity.

Chapter III surveyed the existing research on the effects of using computers to provide instruction. One can conclude from that literature that there are major technological substitution possibilities, but they tend to have different impacts on learning improvement. The most consistent finding from the existing literature is that the most appropriate use of technology under current levels of technological opportunity is for math drill and practice at the upper-elementary and secondary levels. There are, however, a number of major methodological problems with the literature on the effectiveness of computer-based instruction.

One of the major limitations to that literature is the restricted range of instructional objectives that have been researched. Most research at the elementary-secondary level has been geared to the appropriateness of using computers for delivering basic skills. Unfortunately, there is little research on many other potential uses of computers. For example, there are virtually no data on whether, and under what conditions, computer use can stimulate higher-order skills in students. Redfield and Rousseau (1981) conclude that a predominant mode of higher-order questioning techniques in a classroom can stimulate basic skill achievement. Can the same effect be achieved using some of the logic skill software training that has recently become available and the more intelligent forms of software that will be available in the near future? If so, for what kinds of students, and for what modes of use? Likewise, there are few data on the extent to which higher-order skills acquired on the computer are transferrable to more traditional settings and applications, or the integrative processes that are needed to facilitate such transfer.

This leads to a more general question: What kinds of integration mechanisms are needed between teacher and computer use activities, in terms of both student socialization and teacher activities, for all areas of skill development? Baker, Herman, and Yeh (1981) found that the use of traditional games in a classroom detracted from achievement. Would the same finding apply to instructional computer games? If so, in what types of teacher integration activities? Few computer use programs currently found in schools provide careful articulation between the activities on the computer and those in the classroom.

Another problem with existing literature is the tendency to look at computer use from a macro rather than a micro perspective. In other words, researchers usually look for an either-or answer, in global terms, to the question of whether computers work, rather than try to determine the specific instructional tasks and conditions for which they might (or might not be) effective. Partialling out those conditions where computer use is appropriate is further complicated by lax methodological controls. Many important intervening variables, such as the quality of the software and the extent to which the computer instruction activities are coordinated with the traditional curriculum and instruction, are ignored. In addition, technological opportunity is treated as a constant. Hence, a particular application that does not appear to be appropriate using one form of technology is assumed to be inappropriate under newer forms of technology, and/or research is not conducted on the newer forms of technology because they are not widely available (which ignores the likelihood that they will probably be affordable in the near future).

Not only has existing research on technology effectiveness failed to cover many types of instructional interactions and conditions; it has also failed to examine *why* technology is successful in cases where it works. Valid theories on why computer-based instruction works when it does would improve the design of software and would make it possible to predict which types of software are most likely to be effective a priori, thereby helping to direct the research effort and reduce the amount of experimentation needed.

There are a number of possible hypotheses to explain why computer-based instruction can be effective. Tobias (1982) suggests that the primary determinant of whether an instructional approach will be effective is the degree to which it increases student absorption levels. Any educator who observes the intense concentration that arcade games arouse has probably wondered if it would be possible to design educational curricula that could arouse a fraction of that type of absorption. Malone (1981) has been able to isolate at least some of the factors (such as fantasy, scorekeeping, and increasing levels of difficulty) that are key determinants of the degree of absorption. Some software companies are already developing instructional software based on these principles.

Perhaps the early socialization of children, whereby they acquire an increasing percentage of their information from watching television, predisposes early elementary students to expect, and prefer, to learn from electronic images. It may be that the teacher in the classroom who relies on audio communication to transmit information seems as culturally alien to the students as if the individual attempted to communicate in sign language. Hayes, Chemeski, and Birnbaum (1980), in their studies of children's learning from television, found that preschoolers retained more information presented by electronic images than that in the largely audio sections of the show. This suggests that graphic presentation of instructional materials is more likely to increase retention than is reliance on static text. (One program that recently appeared on the market which uses the concept of imaging creatively introduces students to the concept of the sentence by putting on the screen a series of words in random order and a group of objects. If students arrange the words so as to form a sentence, the objects "act out" the sentence's meaning. While watching Judy run may not be much of a turn-on, the approach is likely to facilitate the long-term memory for the concept of sentence.) The study also suggests that as technological opportunity for low-cost, sophisticated computer graphics increases, the instructional processes for which technology is appropriate will also increase.

It is likely too that there is a relationship between the basic learning style/modality of students and the probability that computer-based instruction will be effective. Alternatively, there may be relationships between learning modality and the relative effectiveness of different approaches to constructing software. It may also be that students with different learning modalities will find it easier to learn to program in different languages. For example, Pascal requires more highly structured thinking processes than does Basic. In addition, relationships between classroom process variables, such as methods of grouping and sequencing computer activities, may mediate the effectiveness of a given piece of software.

It also seems likely that certain approaches work better at different grade levels with different types of students. For example, unstructured software (where the child directs the operation of the computer) may work better than drill and practice (where the child reacts to directions given by the computer) with very young (K-4) children. The opposite may be true for older students.

These and many other research questions need to be answered before we can operationalize the concept of a low-leverage delivery system wherein specific types of instructional activities are appropriately (in accordance with the principles in Chapter V) singled out for technological substitution. However, it would be a mistake to view these issues as strictly, or even primarily, as a technology research agenda. The basic question is how best to integrate technology into the operation of a school. It therefore makes little sense to study the technology issue independent of the other processes with which it is to be integrated. *The basic research goal is to improve schools within economic constraints.*

For each question raised here about the uses of technology, there are analogous research traditions and methodological problems for many of the other education and social science disciplines. The problem is whether a framework can be developed for integrating the research needs and agendas for defining appropriate uses of technology with those of the scholarly traditions that focus on improving the more traditional instructional processes. Before such a framework can be developed, however, it is important to review the evolution of school improvement research relative to the traditional structural school processes.

5. LINKING EFFICIENCY EQUITY RESEARCH TO EXISTING
RESEARCH ON SCHOOL IMPROVEMENT

Attempts to link school inputs to learning outputs in the seventies were largely unsuccessful. Such research, usually referred to as production function analysis, seemed to find that there was no systematic relationship between what schools did or spent and student performance (for example, see Averch, 1974). Such research implied that it was impossible systematically to improve schools by increasing resources or manipulating such traditional school variables as teacher quality or teaching methodologies. There were major methodological problems with this research. The primary problem was that the variables tended to represent school or district characteristics (e.g., number of books in the library), and performance data tended to be aggregated at the school or district level. In retrospect, measuring and aggregating the data at a district level makes no sense, since the locus of learning production is the classroom. The activities in the classroom, not the district office, determine whether learning will occur.

The second major problem with the production function research of the seventies was that the input variables were usually quite gross. Teacher quality was measured by the number of academic degrees an individual possessed or years of experience, whereas the academic climate was often measured by the number of books in the library. Such measures, while having the virtue of statistical simplicity, have no real bearing on the actual process of teaching and learning and are poor proxies for the complex variables they purport to measure. An analogous situation would be trying to explain factory productivity by analyzing the number of children sired by the workers.

The production function work of Summers and Wolfe (1977) was a significant departure, in that they collected and analyzed data at the classroom level. They were thus able to find a number of significant relationships between input variables (such as teacher characteristics, student ability, class size, and time in classroom) and student achievement outputs. As important as this study was, however, the input variables considered (years of teaching experience, number of educational degrees, and the like) remained gross and general. There was still no attempt to describe relationships between instructional strategies and process (as inputs) and learning. One more disaggregative step was needed in production function analysis.

As this decade began, the attempts by economists to explain classroom-based outcomes and those of school improvement researchers to analyze instructional processes began to merge, and the synthesis led to a new school of research, hereafter referred to as *microeconomic production function analysis*. The basic presumptions of the microeconomic approach are that it should be possible (a) to specify a set of relationships between mixes of instructional process inputs and learning outputs and (b) to utilize the relationships to develop optimal strategies for investing in particular amounts of particular types of instructional processes. An allied concept is David Berliner's notion of "teacher as executive," in which the teacher is viewed as an individual who, with the help of research, makes time allocation decisions for various mixes of instructional processes.

The methodological issues associated with linking the characteristics of the instructional activities to which students are exposed with their learning achievement are outlined by Dreeben and Thomas (1980). In that edited volume, Harnischfeger and Wiley and Brown and Saks described the feasibility and utility of a microeconomic approach to production function analysis, and Berliner developed a framework for characterizing classroom instructional activities. As previously noted, this new form of school improvement research began to find substantial variations in classroom time allocations for particular instructional processes—variations that have been shown to be related to student outcomes. (Hereafter, the terms *school improvement research* and *microeconomic production function analysis* will be used interchangeably.)

A major flaw remains in this new school of research, however: the acceptance of basic structural sameness as necessarily a political reality. As a result, researchers have attempted to relate differences in learning outcomes to variations of only highly traditional common forms of instructional inputs, such as direct instruction or grouping. For example, when Monk (1981), in his review of the microeconomics literature, notes that "classrooms vary in the degree in which they are

differentiated technologically," he is referring only to highly traditional *social technologies,* such as the method of grouping, which have
very limited potential to increase individualization or the efficiency of
instructional services in general. The use of hard technology is generally not considered within this research tradition.

The issue of how to design a research agenda for defining appropriate uses of computers within a low-leverage delivery system now turns
full circle. Technology effectiveness research tends to ignore related
traditional instructional process variables, while the school improvement research tends to ignore technology use variables. Such differ-
entiation makes little sense, since both schools of research seek the
same end and it is not going to be possible to maximize efficiency
gains without an integration of the two traditions. Most major and
long-lasting efficiency improvements in the history of humankind
have resulted from the mating of a new hard technological capability
with new or modified forms of social technologies. This is as true for
the primitive hunting group as it is for the modern Japanese factory.

Therefore, a research initiative to provide a knowledge base to determine appropriate uses of computers in schools in a low-leverage environment should not be viewed strictly as a technology use research
agenda. Rather, it should be viewed as an integral part of school effectiveness research. The foci of such research would be to study (a) how
the use of high technology can best supplement the efforts of teachers
working in accordance with the latest research on traditional instructional management practices and (b) what kinds of new instructional
management and student socialization practices best integrate the use
of technology into overall instructional objectives. The latter objective
would include generating theory on why various combinations work as
well or as poorly as they do. (Table 11 summarizes the differences in the
research bases needed to support the use of the traditional delivery system and the technology-based ones.)

Such research would have to be carried out for a wide range of
instructional objectives, with varying forms of technology use, and
social integration processes. The goal, consistent with the principles
of microeconomic research, would be to determine optimal technology substitution strategies (across particular sets of instructional areas and objectives) so as to maximize the amount and variety of in-

TABLE 11   Comparison of the Research Implications of the Alternative Forms of Delivery Systems

	Traditional	Low-Leverage	High-Leverage
Fundamental educational unit	School or classroom	Educational activities in classrooms	Courses
School finance	Expenditure and tax equity	Efficiency equity and access equity	Maximizing efficiency through technological substitution
Political analysis	Interest-group lobbying, power structure	Environmental collapse	Environmental collapse
Research base	Macroproduction functions, learning theory, diffusion of innovation, knowledge utilization, interest-group theory	Microlevel production functions, learning theory, artificial intelligence, cost-effectiveness analysis, politics and sociology of automation	Cost-effectiveness analysis, politics and sociology of automation

structional services that can be provided subject to the constraints of available monies and teacher time. (Appendix B contains a more formal statement of the model.)

It remains to be seen what the best strategy would be for the federal government to stimulate the research needed to determine appropriate levels of technological substitution. A separate, new, technology-specific research initiative, isolated from existing NIE research efforts, would probably not be desirable. What would probably be best is the establishment of a multidisciplinary program in which a percentage of existing relevant research efforts, such as those focusing on school finance and school improvement, are earmarked for technology use research and are combined with $5 to $15 million of new research monies (per year for four years) that are under the control of a technology specialist. This pool of funds would then be administered by a panel consisting of a representative of each research area.

It would also be important to relax some federal guidelines and allow a certain percentage of the research funds to be used to purchase technology for placement in research settings. If such research is to be valuable in a policy sense, it must anticipate future, potentially widespread use of a particular type of technological or integrative social process, and it must be conducted prior to its becoming cost-effective. As a result, much of the research must be conducted using technology configurations that do not commonly exist at the time research is undertaken. In a sense, technology use laboratories must be created in schools using technology forms that are still unaffordable by most institutions (even if they already have extensive technology use programs). Thus, the only way such a laboratory can be set up is if the researchers furnish (donate) the technology.

An alternative solution to the problem of obtaining funding for equipment costs for experimental targeted use programs would be for NIE to link researchers with a series of schools interested in funding such costs. As opposed to the planned variation approach utilized in the Follow-Through Program, however, the federal government would not dictate the models or provide the money for establishing the program. Rather, NIE could act as a facilitator between researchers and practitioners to identify the kind of specific learning outcomes and instructional interactions that can be facilitated with intensive use of the current state of technology. It would also be necessary to identify the kinds of structural variation (e.g., number of minutes per day, classroom versus lab) within each proposed use that need to be tested. Existing networks, such as the regional labs and the Urban School Network, could be used to identify districts interested in targeting at least one school to try out a model systematically. NIE could then provide funding for the evaluation of the program and for dissemination of the results.

Such a *voluntary planned variation approach* would require relatively high expenditures in one or several targeted schools within a district, but would still represent a very small percentage of overall computer expenditures within a large district. Such an approach would reverse the trend of large districts to spread their technology dollars in a homogenized low-use mode across all schools, and to emphasize the computer as curriculum rather than as the deliverer of instructional interaction. Such a trend will not provide a systematic data base on how to use technology appropriately. The voluntary planned variation approach would not only generate the knowledge needed to determine how and when to use a given technology by the point in time when the costs of intensive use have dropped substantially, but also would leverage scarce federal research resources. The voluntary planned variation approach would be an ongoing process as new forms of technology appear, and would facilitate physical implementation. Given that most administrators and board members are currently engaged in a genuine search for guidance on how to proceed with the implementation of technology, there would undoubtedly be sufficient numbers of districts (about ten to thirty would be needed) that would be interested in voluntarily participating in such a research effort.

Determining which uses of technology are appropriate is critical for measuring both efficiency equity and access equity.

6. MEASURING ACCESS EQUITY

To what extent is access to appropriate uses of technology equitably distributed? The major obstacle to answering this question at this point is the absence of an adequate knowledge base for defining what constitutes appropriate use. Those who are concerned about access equity tend to address this issue by collecting gross aggregate data such as the number of schools with computers, the number of computers in schools, the average number of computers per student, or the extent to which specialty technology use courses, such as programming or computer literacy, are offered. A particular form of analysis that is quite popular with technologists is to estimate the cost of giving every child a computer. Such definitions of appropriateness are not consistent with the notion that has been advocated in this work and are a throwback to past errors in trying to describe the complexity of the instructional process with gross, almost irrelevant, measures. They are also a throwback to the school finance research of the seventies, which focused primarily on questions related to the distribution of input measures and assumed that equal distribution would substantially narrow the gap in student performance. The issue is not the number of computers in use but the extent to which they are used (successfully) to improve students' basic, higher-order, and computer use skills in an era of constrained resources.

At the same time, while the availability of technology is not a guarantee that it will be used appropriately, availability is a prerequisite. To the extent that it is possible to use data on the acquisition of technology as an indicator of the likelihood that it will be used appropriately (admittedly, a highly questionable assumption), then the data at this point in time are not encouraging as far as access equity is concerned. Two recent surveys (by Market Data Retrieval, 1982, and Quality Education Data, 1982) suggest that the availability of technology in schools may be evolving in such a way that it is inversely related to wealth. For example, the former survey found that 30 percent of schools with less than 5 percent Title I (disadvantaged) students had computers, as compared to only 12 percent of schools with high concentrations of such students. The latter survey found that 32 percent of schools in districts in the upper thirty-fifth percentile of wealth had computers, as compared to only 9 percent of schools in the poorest districts. In addition, the higher the concentration of minorities, the lower the probability that the schools had micros.

These data are, however, changing rapidly. It may be that computer use in poor districts is lagging by only a year and is growing at the same absolute rate as in the richer districts. However, even if the availability of computers is growing at a reasonable rate in the poorer districts, there may be differentials in the management skills that prevent students in such districts from getting access to *appropriate* computer use opportunities to the same extent as students in rich districts with equal numbers of computers. Alternatively, both rich and poor districts may hoard the computers for use essentially by a select group of gifted students.

The alternative possibilities suggest that there is a need for the federal government to monitor the extent to which access to appropriate computer use activities evolves equitably. Such research must look beyond superficial statistics and collect data on the distribution of an instructional use whose appropriateness has been validated by research. For example, it would be important (at the present time) to have data on the extent to which schools provide twenty minutes of daily math CAI for sixth- and eighth-grade students whose performance is more than a year and a half below grade level, as well as the extent to which availability is a function of wealth and race.

7. ALLEVIATING DISPARITIES IN ACCESS EQUITY

If there are inequities in access equity, the key policy question is whether they result from differentials in fiscal capacity or managerial capability. If the former, then there would appear to be justification for federal funding intervention. Such intervention should probably be (a) based on some measure of fiscal capacity, (b) earmarked for the acquisition of technology and related staff development, and (c) provided on a matching fund basis.

The matching fund requirement is important because it is unlikely that, in the absence of some district commitment to the use of technology, external funding will have significant impact on the instructional program. In the absence of district interest (as reflected in a budgetary commitment) in computers, technology that is simply dumped into the district is unlikely to arouse significant curricular reform. Without prior district initiative, externally funded technology will end up in the closet or as the province of a few students and teachers. Matching fund requirements are also reasonable, because (as noted in Chapter V) the costs for technology use are sufficiently small that any district that wants to can get some effort under way within existing resources.

Such funding should also be provided on a multiyear basis to discourage districts from buying loads of equipment in one fell swoop. Rather, the pattern of funding should be consistent with the phasing-in patterns discussed in Chapter V, wherein the establishment of the program occurs in a manner consistent with the schedules for staff development and changes in technological opportunity. In addition, it should be required that a certain percentage of the grants must be used to acquire software; otherwise districts will use the funds to load up on hardware. Ideally, districts would be given an initial planning grant to identify the software they wish to purchase, and would be required to develop a plan for linking the software to instructional objectives in order to receive the major portion of the funding.

There is also a need to provide some support for staffing. Although districts typically can afford to begin the process of acquiring equipment, it is usually impossible for most districts to hire additional teachers under existing budgetary constraints. It is therefore difficult for them to hire technical specialists (even if they can find them). Although most existing staff can be trained to use software for remediation and reinforcement activities (see Tables 8 and 9 in Chapter V), computer use skill activities (e.g., programming) require a higher degree of technical competence to teach. There are already technical specialists at the high school level, but it is more difficult to work computer use activities into the curriculum at the elementary level. For this reason, the first (and probably only) priority for using any of these funds for staffing should be to hire traveling technical specialists at the elementary level. The primary function of these personnel would be to provide computer use skills to students in several (four or five) schools. Alternatively, staffing funds could be used to fund some nontraditional types of staff at the elementary level (such as college students who would serve as teaching assistants) to provide the computer use skills. (This type of program is discussed in detail in Chapter VII.)

Finally, some of the funds would have to be allocated for general staff development geared toward getting the typical teacher ready to operate the basic kinds of software.

If, on the other hand, inequities emerge that are the result of differences between the willingness or abilities of administrators in poorer districts and those in richer districts to harness the capabilities of technology, external funding for the acquisition will again have little impact on the curriculum. In such a situation it may be appropriate for the federal government to attempt to stimulate the availability of technology in such communities by relying on non-public school mechanisms. One possibility would be to provide funding for technology centers in neighborhood libraries. Another would be to offer tax credits to businesses that provide on-the-job training to the poor. A modified voucher scheme could encourage schools (public as well as private) with technologically relevant curricula to recruit students from poor families. A final alternative would be to expand and equalize access to home-based delivery systems by requiring television manufacturers to include microprocessor chips in their sets (much as the government currently requires a UHF receiver). While such policies may help the onset of environmental collapse, there might not be a realistic alternative for providing the poor with access to instruction that gives them an equal chance to participate in the information economy.

It is estimated that the cost of such a program would be $100 to $300 million per year for four to five years. Such monies would be sufficient to help fund ten technology stations per year in 10,000 schools, along with staff development, software and 2,000 to 3,000 elementary-level traveling resource teachers.

The programs in this section are recommended for reducing foreseeable disparities in access equity. However, the federal government might decide that it is in the national interest to accelerate the widespread use of technology in all schools. The policy implications of such an eventuality are explored in the next section.

8. ECONOMIC EMERGENCY RATIONALE PROGRAMS

It is impossible to predict at this point what the future of the economy will be. If conditions worsen and unemployment increases or remains at high levels, the federal government will be forced to intervene with new programs or policy approaches. To the extent that there is a mismatch between the skill needs of the information economy and the skills available in the work force, and the imbalance is, or is perceived to be, a major depressant on our international competitive standing and overall economic growth, there will be a need (or pressure) to enact crash educational programs as one part of the solution. Such a rationale is hereafter referred to as the "economic emergency" rationale. While the previously recommended programs would remain a top priority under such a rationale, there would be a need to consider additional interventions.

While a major component of a federal education program enacted under this rationale would be to retrain laid-off workers, there would probably also be demands to improve the technological relevance of the school curriculum—at all levels. At the university level, this would require subsidizing salaries so that universities could compete for beginning Ph.Ds in technical areas where there are teachers shortages. It would also be important to subsidize the quality of professional life in academia for such individuals by providing support for travel, modern equipment, and sabbaticals. Likewise, the federal government would have to continue supporting a few key installations of very expensive state-of-the-art equipment (observatories, linear accelerators, fusion reactors, and so on) that are available to the academic community at large.

The community college systems are relatively new, but it can be expected that the technology available on those campuses will soon begin to obsolesce. In addition, community colleges face many of the same personnel problems as the other levels of education. To the extent that rates of obsolescence and availability of qualified personnel to staff the technology areas are a function of wealth or ethnicity, there could also be problems of access equity at this level.

This would be particularly debilitating, since the community college systems are likely to bear a major share of retraining activities. The most intelligent policies at this level would favor some form of differential salary subsidies and technology acquisition grants. If systematic problems of access equity do appear, it may be important to allocate such grants based on the fiscal capacities of the institutions.

The problems at the elementary and secondary levels, however, are more severe and more deeply ingrained. For reasons that are discussed in the next chapter, it is unlikely that differential pay subsidies will solve the staffing problems. The argument has already been made that the only approach with any potential for being a solution requires that highly traditional organizations adopt new forms of delivery systems and begin to change the nature of their work.

The only additional policy change that would be recommended under the economic emergency rationale is to expand the scope of the programs suggested for the access equity rationale—that is, such assistance would be allocated on a more widespread basis. The criteria already discussed (i.e., preplanning, multiyear funding, software acquisition requirements, and some form of fund matching) should be maintained. The only difference would be that fiscal capacity would not play the key role in determining funding (although it could play a role in matching requirements). The cost of such a program for the elementary-secondary level would probably be $200 to $600 million per year for four to five years.

The major difference implied by the economic emergency rationale is the recognition or formalization of the development of more technologically relevant forms of schools as a national priority. The federal government might seek to leverage whatever funding it provided in this area to induce states to adopt appropriate response policies as well. The notion of the federal government imposing its will is not likely to receive much enthusiasm in Washington or the states, but it must be recognized that if a national priority of developing more technologically relevant schools is to be attained, it is also necessary for states to adopt a number of nontraditional policies—ones that are not likely to be popular with powerful statewide educational interest groups. (The specific types of state policies that would be needed are discussed in Chapter VII.) This suggests the need for some form of intergovernmental pressure.

The issue of intergovernmental pressure is not a simple matter of black-and-white differentiations between categorical aid and general aid. As Kutner and Sherman (1982) note, many different kinds and degrees of control can be exerted from the federal level. It would probably be most appropriate if the federal government did not mandate the existence of certain programs, but rather required only that states pass legislation eliminating legal constraints that now prevent school districts that wish to do so from implementing some of the nontraditional reforms. At that point, grass-roots pressure, surfacing as predicted around 1985, would take care of the rest. It is not necessary for the federal government to wield a club—only a twig—and only when and if it becomes clear that national economic survival is truly at stake.

9. LEGISLATIVE INITIATIVES

In addition to funding for each of the proposals in this chapter, there are a number of other, low-cost legislative initiatives that should be considered. Bits and pieces of legislation for existing programs must be reformed in order to make it easier to integrate those objectives with technology use concerns. For example, some definitions of vocational education must be reconsidered with respect to both the kinds of skill training that are approved and the kinds of students who are enrolled. Maybe vocational funds should be used to offer advanced programming classes at the high school level, even if most of the students would be going on to college. We may also need to respecify funding priorities within the existing vocational skill areas.

Other federal rules and regulations must be examined to determine whether they are dysfunctional for helping schools initiate appropriate uses of computers in a low-leverage mode. One example, already mentioned, is allowing portions of research grants to be used to purchase and install state-of-the-art equipment and applications in school settings for experimental purposes. There are probably many other programs in which it might be useful to drop some restrictions against using funds for technology-related capital acquisitions (on a limited, temporary basis and using appropriate safeguards).

It is also important at this point in time to begin thinking about a federal role in stimulating either a high-leverage delivery system or composite delivery systems. Such involvement would almost certainly need to focus on improving schools' access to highband telecommunication systems. Options would include (a) subsidizing district use of information utilities, (b) subsidizing district hookups to local cable or state networks, and (c) subsidizing a federal satellite, or channels on existing satellites, for educational broadcasting. Unfortunately, the whole cost and regulatory structure (not to mention the technology itself) of the telecommunication field is changing too rapidly at this point. It is difficult to recommend a policy other than the copout that the issue should be kept under advisement. What is clear, however, is that the technological opportunities for these alternative delivery systems will increase rapidly after mid-decade.

10. SUMMARY

In this chapter it has been suggested that federal policy should maintain a dual focus. The first need is to provide support to remove market impediments to (a) the development of highly automated intelligent software by a crash R & D program and (b) the marketing of high-quality conventional software via an entrepreneurial support program. The second need is for a multidisciplinary research program designed to operationalize the concept of "appropriate" computer use by determining the types of instruction. The research and policy question is not, Is technology effective? but rather, *Is technology cost-effective for delivering a particular type of micro-level instructional interaction?* The basic goal is to prepare the knowledge base needed to utilize technological forms that become available in appropriate ways within as short a time span as possible from the time that the opportunity for such use emerges.

Research is also needed to monitor whether there is any wealth-related disparity in how the distribution of access to needed technology-based instructional opportunities evolves. If such access appears to evolve in an unequitable manner, federal support for the acquisition of technology would probably be needed. Specific guidelines have been proposed for avoiding the simple dumping of hardware on dis-tricts that are ill-equipped to use them appropriately.

Proposals also have been presented for a wider federal involvement, should it be determined that such a role is in the federal interest. This is not to argue that such involvement is absolutely necessary. *What is absolutely true, however, is that in the absence of the software stimulation and research generation proposals, federal funding efforts to stimulate the development of technologically relevant curricula, and the use of low-leverage systems in education, are likely to fail.* Simply throwing money at the problem will not solve it. The availability of technology without a curricular theory on how to use it is of no value.

Table 12 contains a summary of policy recommendations. While the recommended policy initiatives would require new funding, the amounts proposed are relatively modest as compared to the efficiency gains they could generate. In addition, the proposals are relatively mod-est as compared to typical proposals, which simply focus on the provi-sion of massive amounts of hardware for school districts. The top-prior-ity proposals, which are needed either to stimulate the adoption of low-leverage systems without massive federal intervention or to in-crease the probability of the success of such intervention, are estimated to cost only $31 to $47 million per year—as opposed to hundreds of millions and billions for other federal efforts in education, most of which do not promise to meet emerging educational needs.

In addition, the top-priority recommendations are designed to in-terface with a series of state-level policy initiatives. The next chapter explores what the state role should be and recommends individual and joint state policy initiatives.

TABLE 12   Recommended Federal Policy Initiatives for Low-Leverage Systems

Problem	Proposed Program	Time Frame	Estimated Cost
Inadequate knowledge*	(a) Research on defining appropriate uses of technology (voluntary planned variation approach)	1984-88	$5-15 million/year of new money plus a share of some of the existing research efforts
	(b) Research on determining the degree of access equity	1984-86	$250,000/year
Removing market impediments to software availability*	(a) R & D program to support development of intelligent software	1984-89	$20-30 million/year
	(b) Entrepreneurial support to increase supply of quality software	1984-89	$1-2 million/year
Emerging disparities of access equity**	Fund acquisition of software and hardware in schools (or other agencies) elementary level resource teachers	1984-88	$100-300 million/year
Economic emergency**	Fund acquisition of software and hardware in schools (or other agencies) elementary level resource teachers	1984-88	$200-600 million/year

*top priority
**conditional priority

VII IMPLICATIONS FOR STATE POLICY

THE STATE ROLE in removing obstacles to technological relevancy in schools must be differentiated from that of the federal government. Whereas the federal role is conceptualized as removing national impediments through basic research and entrepreneurial support activities, the state role is viewed as removing those obstacles that are local and regional. This chapter describes appropriate fiscal incentives and legislative initiatives to deal with (a) shortages in the availability of highly automated (nonintelligent) software; (b) inadequate supplies of trained technical personnel, such as math and science teachers; and (c) the lack of knowledge on the part of local districts about how to establish appropriate programs or how to identify quality software. There is also a need to remove barriers to appropriate use of high technology in education imposed or tolerated by traditional accounting and certification requirements.

Given the strained fiscal capability of most states, policies that can be implemented at relatively low cost will be emphasized. In addition, policy initiatives that are essentially local and hence should be dealt with on an individual state basis will be distinguished from those that should be implemented on a regional or multistate basis.

166

1. INCREASING THE SUPPLY OF HIGH-QUALITY SOFTWARE

While the previous chapter dealt primarily with the need to develop more intelligent software, there is also a need to increase the supply of high-quality, automated nonintelligent software. There are actually two problems with the availability of the latter. The first is the quantity. The second relates to the form in which existing software is provided. Although some bemoan the fact that there is no good software available, such is not the case. There is quite a bit of certain kinds of quality software, but it is usually provided in a highly nonautomated form.

The two major factors inhibiting an increase in the availability of high-quality nonintelligent software are (a) the desire of publishers not to dilute their profits from the highly competitive textbook market and (b) the perceived limited market for educational software. The latter results from publishers' skepticism about whether schools will be willing to make major investments in technology and educators will be sufficiently sophisticated to want to spend the money needed to purchase high-quality software for the equipment that they do purchase. In addition, the piracy problem further restricts the size of the potential market.

While the previous chapter suggested that the development of intelligent software is an appropriate goal for the federal government, given the highly technical nature of the supporting R & D effort required, there is also a need for greater quantities of highly automated nonintelligent software. States can support the development of software through three techniques. First, states can help create markets for software. Second, they can contract, either individually or jointly, for the development of specific types of software. Finally, a consortium of states, particularly those that have textbook adoption lists, can encourage, or coerce, publishers to produce software that conforms to a set of standards. (See Appendix C for a list of recommended standards.) The major leverage that such a group has, other than professional suasion, is the threat to withdraw the texts of nonconforming publishers from the approved textbook lists in their states.

The first approach, the creation of a market, derives from the classic chicken-and-egg problem. If educators do not buy software, developers will not produce it. If educators buy the cheapest rather than the best software available, low-quality software is what will be supplied. In the absence of inexpensive good software, educators will tend to limit their investment to the purchase and use of computers, thereby limiting the potential future educational software market. As a result, the *first priority* for any funding or tax credit initiatives should be to provide districts with resources to acquire, or obtain donations of, *software*. It makes little sense for public funds to be used to subsidize hardware acquisition or donation, since that segment of the computer industry is flush and experiencing escalating sales. Hardware production does not need public support to survive, innovate, and continue to reduce costs. The imperatives of free market competition in the private sector will be sufficient to do that. While hardware has the private sector to support its development, educational software has no external market other than education.

It has already been suggested that the federal government could increase the supply of basic software by providing entrepreneurial assistance to emerging software companies. If state government wishes to subsidize the creation or expansion of an educational software market, the best way would probably be to provide a certain level of assistance on a per-student basis with some matching fund requirement, or to provide such assistance as a percentage of a district's hardware or software acquisition budget. Such an approach would signal to software developers that there will be a stable market in which to compete while also stimulating increased district investment.

States must remove legislative constraints in order to give districts more flexibility in applying their own funds toward the acquisition of software. States tend to differ in whether they view software as either a capital outlay item or part of the operations budget. States should give districts the option of financing software acquisition from either portion of their budget. In addition, in those states that provide funds for the acquisition of textbooks, districts should be allowed to apply a percentage of those funds toward software acquisition. Although textbook publishers could be expected to oppose such legislation, it makes sense to view the computer as a curricular device—a dynamic form of the book.

States can also stimulate the software market by formally contracting for the development of specific types of software. This can be done by states acting either on their own or through a consortium. Given the high cost of software development, the latter approach probably makes more sense if a common set of needs and specifications can be worked out. It would be folly, however, for states to try to develop those forms of software that require extensive R & D efforts, since they do not have the technical expertise to oversee such projects. Hence, it makes little sense to envision states funding the development of video disk-based intelligent software. What probably makes the most sense is for states to support software projects that can be comfortably implemented within existing technology and that have high and immediate payoffs, both fiscally and educationally. The highest payoff, along with the greatest probability of success, would probably come from applications in the cost-saving category in Table 6 (Chapter 5): driver-training simulations and science laboratory experiments, for example. Additional candidates for state software development projects could be courseware for advanced science and math courses (to cope with personnel shortages) and the conversion of quality minicomputer software to operate on micros.

Focusing and limiting state efforts in software development do not guarantee success. Federal efforts at software contracting have heretofore been notably unsuccessful. The U.S. Government Accounting Office (1979) performed an audit of nine federally sponsored software development projects and found that of the $6.8 million spent, only $317,000 (or 5 percent) of the effort resulted in software that was eventually usable. Software development contract management is not a simple process. The most notable success in state software development projects to date has been the Minnesota Educational Computer Consortium (MECC), where state funds were used to refine a wide variety of instructional software that is now marketed nationally. MECC's efforts, which consisted largely of producing a series of discrete simulations for the Apple computer, were successful largely because they were not overly ambitious.

While the MECC experience suggests that it is feasible to envision a limited state role in software development, *it clearly makes no sense to suggest that all governmental software development efforts should become the responsibility of the states.* While the view that all necessary software development projects not currently supported by industry should be delegated to the states is consistent with the philosophy of new federalism, such policy is unrealistic. There is a need (as discussed in the previous chapter) to differentiate which aspects of software development states can indeed take responsibility for, given limitations on expertise and resources. In addition, given the rapid increase in the number of companies capable of producing nonintelligent forms of education software, *it is not clear that there is a need for states to get directly involved in any software development activities.* Such direct involvement should probably be a lower priority for the states than the other software stimulation strategies being suggested, and should probably be used only as a last resort.

The final step states can take to stimulate the development of software is to pressure the major educational publishers. Such pressure could take many forms, ranging from suggestions to threats. Probably more important than the nature of the pressure is an understanding of the software needs and problems by state-level educators and legislators, and the formation of a united coalition of these individuals to address the problems systematically. The key problems that need to be addressed by such a coalition include (a) how to develop more appropriate pricing and general marketing policies and (b) how to develop standards of desirable software characteristics. The latter would include recommendations for software content as well as automation characteristics.

There is clearly a need to reform pricing policies. Existing policies, which usually consist of charging for each copy of a program, discourage the purchase and use of multiple copies of programs—which limits student access to the interactions provided. This type of pricing policy also encourages piracy—which again limits the potential market and thereby limits development. In an attempt to limit the potential for piracy and unauthorized use, publishers often refuse to provide backup copies of software, or at least make it inconvenient to obtain spare copies. This, of course, makes it inconvenient for schools to use the software. A middle-ground approach to breaking this circular problem is to encourage licensing policies wherein a manufacturer agrees to allow a school or district to make as many copies of the program as it needs for its own use in return for payment of a flat fee that is somewhere between the single-copy cost and the cost for all the copies that a district would need.

Another licensing approach would be for a state to guarantee a given publisher an agreed-upon amount of revenue in return for licensing the state education agency to make as many copies of the program as needed for the state's schools. While this proposal would require state agencies to get into the business of making copies of software, much of the cost would be recouped through sales to school districts (assuming that the agency has wisely selected the software that it will make available). This is no different than what some state agencies already do to facilitate the dissemination of curriculum guides and videotapes. The major drawback of this approach is that it requires the state department to make guesses about the size of the potential market for a particular program—a time-consuming process in which errors could be very expensive to the state. A better alternative would be to allow the state department to make copies as needed and pay on a per copy basis.

Probably the most creative licensing arrangement to date is that of MECC. MECC currently sells a state membership for a one-time fee of $10,000. Districts in the states that pay this fee can then get copies of these popular programs at substantially reduced prices and can make as many copies as they need. However, such licensing policies, while terrific for educators, limit potential sales to such a degree that few publishers are likely to adopt similar ones, as opposed to more traditional forms of agreements.

Generally, then, licensing arrangements simplify the marketing process for publishers—particularly where state contracts are involved. Selling and policing costs are reduced for the vendors, thereby increasing the profitability of software production. This would be of particular benefit to small software companies. To the extent that such savings all passed on to the user, the licensing process would make it easier for districts to use good software in a comprehensive way. It would also protect the major publishing companies against the possibility of large numbers of districts investing heavily in microcomputers and using textbook funds to acquire software. The major publishers, under present marketing policies, might find themselves left out in the cold if districts began to seek software from other sources, using funds traditionally earmarked for their products to pay for the software.

At the same time, failure to establish a tradition of licensing agreements would also hurt education. It now appears that technology may begin to get the upper hand on piracy. Incorporating segments of programs on read-only memory (ROM) chips or providing software on video disks will make it difficult to make copies of programs without very large capital investments. (It currently costs about $10,000 to produce a video disk.) If publishers are forced to put their software on such high-capital-intensive devices to recoup their investments, it will be difficult to convince them to go along with licensing schemes, and schools will find it difficult to obtain adequate numbers of copies of popular programs. The increasing capital requirements will probably force small companies out of the education market, which will have the net effect of reducing the supply of software.

There is also a need for a coalition of state-level officials to adopt a position on desired software characteristics. It is fairly easy to define a set of general expectations about what will be considered unacceptable software. (See Appendix C for a list of desirable software characteristics.) A number of organizations that evaluate educational software, such as EPIE and MICROSIFT, have already developed criteria for assessing quality. It is also easy to describe those educational activities for which software would be desired. A less discussed problem is the form in which software is provided.

Almost all existing high-quality software is provided on limited-storage media such as floppy disks or cassettes. This results in difficult-to-manage, highly fragmented programs. For example, most of the k-7 CAI programs require four to eight disks per micro (or every third computer) to provide the entire curriculum, and extra disks are needed to store student progress information. Backup or multiple copies are required for each disk. As a result, it can take thirty to sixty disks, or cassettes, just to provide math remediation activities in a school. Finding the right disk for the identified student need, and switching between program and management disks, is inconvenient and messy. These required noninstructional interventions reduce the automation potential and benefits of the system.

The alternative to having related program segments on multiple floppy disks is to make the (same) software available on a hard disk network. This would be cheaper for schools than putting floppy drives on each microcomputer, and the high storage capacity of the hard disk would make it possible to put all the programs used on a single storage device and make them automatically available to any of the micro-computer stations. The programs would operate faster and without logistical interventions. The realized automation would thus go up as overall hardware costs go down. In addition, the costs of converting most software to hard disk would not be very substantial for vendors. Assuming that an appropriate licensing agreement could be worked out so that districts paid no more for the hard disk version of the soft-ware than for the same number of floppy disk copies that they would otherwise have had to buy, everyone would benefit. Unfortunately, it may still not be done.

Three factors are likely to inhibit the availability of hard disk ver-sions of popular software. The first is simply inertia based on igno-rance. The second is the chicken-and-egg problem, wherein pub-lishers do not convert elementary-level software because elementary districts do not have hard disks, and the schools do not buy the hard disks because there is no educational software that will run on them. The third problem is that the publishers have to guess which hard disk networks will be most widely used by schools and must be able to work out satisfactory licensing agreements with that disk vendor. (This latter requirement is necessary if the school is to buy the disk with the software already on it.) Given the many brands of hard disks and available networks, the wrong decision could severely limit sales. Fortunately, one hard disk network is emerging as the predominantly used one at the high school level, and this network has the advantage of being able to handle most of the popular microcomputers.

The following is an actual example of what happens when outstand-ing software is not marketed in a cost-effective, highly automated fashion. The most widely used minicomputer CAI software has just been converted to run on microcomputers. This is the software for which the most extensive research validation exists. Unfortunately, each microcomputer must have its own double-sided floppy disk (with a storage capacity of .5 million characters or .5 MB) at a cost of $1,500. This means that for six CAI stations, a school would have to pay $9,000 for 3 MB of storage on a relatively unreliable medium when a 5 MB highly reliable hard disk can be obtained for $2,000. Since the individual micros are not interconnected, management reports have to be printed out separately from each machine. As a result, if six students are simultaneously pulled out from the same class to work at six CAI stations, the teacher has to analyze six different printouts in order to pull together a composite report of the students—a very nonautomated, unappetizing, and unnecessary prospect.

This and other examples suggest that there is tremendous potential (a) to enhance the effectiveness, (b) to increase the automation, and (c) to reduce the cost of using available quality software, by simply changing the form in which software is available. Doing so would not be a very costly or technically esoteric process. Unfortunately, individual districts do not have sufficient leverage to pressure the publishing companies to change. States must therefore adopt a unified lobbying position for the principle that software costing more than a given amount should be made available in both floppy disk and networked hard disk versions. An alternative to lobbying would be to set aside a certain amount of state funds to assist elementary schools in purchasing hard disks when and if the publishers make their software available on that medium. The assurance of at least some market for such software might encourage publishers to convert their software.

The mere fact that large numbers of state officials have agreed upon a common set of software goals would signal to the publishing industry a growing sophistication among educators that would have to be taken into account in their product offerings. The next level of action would be for states to organize a common, nationally accessible software evaluation data base that would provide information on the extent to which major software packages conform to the articulated software goals. Going even further, educators could circulate warnings against those programs deemed to be undesirable.

The final level of coordinated action would be for states with text-book adoption processes to eliminate from consideration all the texts of publishers who have refused to provide quality software for deliver-ing the same educational activities. Formal coercion, however, would be the least desirable and, one would hope, unnecessary level of action, since such formal censorship can, once unleashed, be used to pursue socially undesirable ends.

A combined strategy of stimulative and punitive actions on the part of state officials seems to be the fairest to all parties and the one most likely to succeed in increasing the supply of quality software. *Failure by top state officials to address the software issue seriously and in a coordinated way will likely result in publishers making low-quality software available to schools and focusing their more creative efforts on marketing educational software for the home.* CBS is already pre-paring to market instructional software to the home. Given the number of homes relative to the number of schools, such a marketing strategy makes obvious business sense. If quality software makers give up on schools, this would probably facilitate environmental collapse—or would at least promote growing public dissatisfaction with reliance on schooling strategies that do not provide capabilities equivalent to what parents can deliver on their own in the home.

2. PROVIDING TECHNICALLY TRAINED PERSONNEL: A CRITIQUE OF EXISTING PROPOSALS

The national shortages of math and science teachers at the second-ary level have already been documented. The most serious inhibitor of the development of a technologically relevant curriculum is the lack of any technical facility among the nonmath and nonscience teachers and the traditional lack of emphasis on developing higher-order skills in the typical classroom curriculum. This creates a particular problem at the elementary level, where large percentages of the generalist staff are mathphobics.

There are a number of proposed solutions to the problem of inade-quate numbers of technical specialists and inadequate levels of techni-cal expertise among the general staff. The most common ones are (a) differential pay to make teaching more attractive to individuals with technical backgrounds, (b) voucher proposals, (c) coöperative ventures with industry, (d) inservice to raise the math and technical competence of existing teachers, and (e) college scholarships for those individuals training to become math teachers. Guthrie and Zussman (1982) provide an excellent overview of these proposals.

Unfortunately, it is difficult to envision any of these working, either separately or jointly, in a healthy economy. Under no circumstances is it conceivable that there are enough public funds to pay a salary differential high enough that the salaries for math and science teachers would be comparable to what industry would offer such individuals. The shortage of teachers in engineering schools and computer science departments, despite differential salaries, is a case in point. Even if it were feasible to raise the salaries for math and science teachers at the secondary level substantially, the only impact would be to stimulate industry to increase its pay scales. The net result of this salary inflation would be higher costs for the schools without a substantial increase in available technical personnel. *Education simply cannot outbid industry for those people the private sector needs and wants.*

Would differential pay, combined with offers of free tuition, encourage existing teachers to take additional coursework in math and science in order to become qualified to teach in those areas? This approach would probably encourage some teachers to make a switch, but it is hard to envision such a program generating anywhere near the numbers needed. The problem here lies with the assumption that increased pay is a successful way to increase the retention of existing staff. Data collected by Victor and Schlechty (1982) suggest otherwise. Their research (discussed in Chapter IV) found that during the mid-seventies, when teacher salaries were rising rapidly, the retention rate of teachers in the upper quartile of ability (as measured by standardized test scores) actually declined. While these data say something about the relative attractiveness of the conditions of teaching, they also suggest that once the brighter teachers have marketable options outside education, they are likely to take advantage of them—regardless of salary incentives.

In other words, the shortage of math and science teachers has to be corrected within the context of higher (academic) ability teachers (in all subject areas) leaving teaching. Therefore, even if salary differential programs were to succeed in inducing large numbers of individuals to switch fields at the secondary level, the result could be a massive Peter Principle phenomenon wherein good social studies and English teachers become mediocre math teachers, and in which math classes are covered at the expense of the quality of the program in the other subject areas. Moreover, it is difficult to envision differential pay solving the problem of inadequate technical background among teachers at the elementary level, where student attitudes toward and competencies in math, science, and logic are first formed. It is not very likely that any inservice program yet designed could turn the majority of these teachers into creative math teachers.

Some districts have recently reported that pay differential programs enabled them to increase their numbers of math and science teachers. Such cases, however, often appear to represent recruitment of such teachers away from other districts that cannot afford to match the salary offers of the pay differential districts. In other words, present pay differential efforts tend to result in a redistribution rather than a net increase in the number of math and science teachers. Voucher plans present the same problem. While the competitive aspects of a voucher system might cause some schools to increase the quality of math and science programs and compete aggressively for available technical personnel, it is difficult to see how a voucher per se will result in a net increase in available teaching personnel with technical skills. Redistributing available technical personnel through either a voucher or a pay differential scheme is likely to introduce major disparities in technological access equity, disparities that probably would be largely a function of wealth.

As a result, barring a depression that greatly restricts the highly technical jobs available in the private sector, it is hard to see how pay differential proposals are going to solve the dual problem of teacher shortages and the lack of technical expertise among elementary school teachers. Such proposals are likely, at the very least, to generate resentment among the staff and are also likely to be formally opposed by teacher unions. As a result, it does not seem to make any sense for states to mandate a pay differential plan. It may make sense to clear legal obstacles at the state level to allow those districts that voluntarily choose to do so to implement a pay differential scheme. Such a step should, however, probably be taken only in states with high degrees of interdistrict equity to avoid the problem of the rich outbidding the poor for math and science teachers.

For those who see industry as a major part of the solution, there is really little incentive for industry to provide massive amounts of assistance to the public schools. While there is a tradition of some companies making personnel available to teach some classes, the occasional volunteer is not likely to make a major dent in the problem. Tucker (1982b) has noted that it makes more economic sense for industry to skim off the best students and establish in-house training programs for them. Moreover, the first priority for any educational involvement on the part of industry in education would probably be at the university level, where there could be some clear reciprocal benefits. For example, IBM recently announced a $50 million donation program to help a series of institutions upgrade their engineering programs.

This does not mean that educators should ignore the potential value of increased industry involvement in education. Programs wherein companies adopt a school are extremely beneficial. State laws that place barriers in the way of classroom volunteers or cash donations from industry should clearly be removed. It is difficult to imagine, however, that such programs by themselves can solve the problem.

To the extent that states make funds available for increasing the capabilities of schools to provide a more technologically relevant curriculum, teacher unions, universities, and most other established educational interest groups can be expected to lobby for applying such monies to inservice training activities. The problem with this traditional approach is that the support mechanisms are not in place. Who is supposed to provide the training? Few colleges of education have technology programs or specialists in math and science education. A survey of 134 southeastern education colleges and universities by *Electronic Education* (1982) found that only 15.5 percent provided a preservice course on training students to use microcomputers. As colleges begin to jump on the bandwagon and offer courses, the question remains of how likely they are to be of high quality. Nor do most state departments or county offices have skilled consultants in these areas. It becomes even more difficult to visualize how inservice can increase the technical capabilities of the mass of generalists or improve their ability to deliver higher-order skills.

The traditional strategy of inservice is not likely to make a substantial dent in the problem, given the nontraditional nature of the skills that need to be delivered. The inservice infrastructure, though compellingly powerful politically, is not equipped to deal with this problem. Unfortunately, most states that try to increase the technological relevance of their schools will probably bow to tradition and put their faith in a combination of inservice and financial incentives to obtain needed training and personnel. Alternatively, states will probably rely strictly on financial incentives to encourage more math and science majors to become teachers. Kentucky, for example, has decided to try the latter strategy and will offer scholarships to individuals who train to become math and science teachers. The success of this approach remains to be seen.

The key point, however, is not that the approaches discussed in this section have no merit, but only that they cannot, by themselves, begin to solve the structural problems that are emerging. Alternative policies must be considered.

3. ALTERNATIVE PROPOSALS FOR PROVIDING TRAINED PERSONNEL

There are at least three alternative strategies for correcting teacher shortages that would get around the problem of substantively retraining current personnel or having to rely on low-probability strategies, such as salary differential programs, vouchers, industry cooperation, and the others discussed in the previous section. The alternatives include (a) career differential programs, in the form of a teaching assistant and a teacher corp program; (b) increasing dependence on technology; and (c) telecommunicated instruction.

The first strategy would be to solve the shortage of available personnel the same way that universities do. Universities typically do not have sufficient faculty to staff substantial portions of undergraduate classes.

The solution is to create a relatively inexpensive category of teacher called the "teaching assistant." Rather than subsidizing hardware vendors or an ossified inservice establishment, it seems to make more sense to subsidize college students—particularly at a point in time when many of their traditional sources of revenue are declining. It would be a simple matter to provide funding to college students who have completed a year of calculus (regardless of their major)—a stipend plus free tuition at a state institution to go into the public schools and teach math or science for a given number of hours per week under the supervision of a regular teacher. Such a teacher assistantship program could produce fifteen to twenty hours a week of highly enthusiastic math and science instruction at a cost of $3,000 to $4,000—approximately a third to a quarter the cost of hiring a conventional teacher.

A variation on the teaching assistant approach would be a program modeled after the Peace Corps which hereafter will be referred to as the teacher corps. Under this proposed program, students would be allowed to teach math and science after completing the sophomore year for up to two years at a beginning teacher's salary. Again, this would cost a lot less, and would be less threatening to the existing staff at a school, than a salary differential program. However, it is highly unlikely that teacher's unions would support a student assistantship or teacher corps program.

If career differential programs such as the teaching assistant and teacher corps proposals are as politically difficult as salary differential programs, and more so than pure inservice strategies, why are they a desirable option for policymakers? First, they are relatively low-cost options. Second, they offer substantial educational advantages over salary differential and inservice approaches.

The first educational advantage is that the career differential programs would attract groups of high-ability students into the schools (assuming that they would not be required to add more than one basic education course to their programs). While such students would probably not be interested in teaching as a career, the present cutbacks in student aid would make the teacher assistant and teacher corps programs very attractive options for high-ability undergraduates. They would also provide a way to bring new and fresh perspectives into public schools (even if on a temporary basis) at a time when the average age of teaching staffs is increasing and their academic skill levels are apparently decreasing.

The second potential educational benefit is that the student assistant and teacher corps programs could stimulate increased interest in math and science among undergraduates. While being a math or science major should not be a requirement to participate in these programs, a certain percentage of available funds should probably be earmarked for students planning to embark on careers in math and science. (It seems to make more sense to use public funds to subsidize such students rather than Apple, Tandy, Atari, and the like, or to invest funds to turn mathphobics into teachers capable of developing linear logic skills in children.)

The third potential educational benefit is that the use of younger, enthusiastic personnel could turn into an interesting form of compensatory program. Summers and Wolfe (1977) found that performance among minority students was inversely related to the experience level of their instructors (i.e., minority students learned more from the younger teachers), while the opposite was true for high-ability students. This, of course, suggests that participants in career differential programs should be placed primarily in high-minority schools. The program participants could also be used to teach computer-related skills to high-ability students, since they would really be training the students to learn in a self-service mode rather than delivering the instructional interactions themselves. In addition, the computer is rapidly becoming part of the culture of the young, and it therefore makes sense to expect the relatively young to have the most credibility with the young in this field.

The second alternative to the reliance on inservice techniques or financial incentives for existing teachers to become math and science teachers is an increased reliance on the diffusion of technology to deliver instructional services. Again, it is probably much easier to train a teacher to show students how to use high-quality problem-solving software than it is to train average teachers to deliver those services themselves. In other words, *it is no longer necessary to train teachers to teach all that the schools will be expected to teach.* For example, if the public suddenly demanded that schools teach Boolean algebra to second- and third-graders, the traditional inservice and training institutions would gear up to teach existing and future teachers Boolean algebra, without any reasonable probability of success. There is, on the other hand, a program called Rocky's Boots that "teaches" young children the formal principles of logic used in the design of electronic circuits. Teachers can learn to show students how to use this program with about twenty minutes of practice. While this example is admittedly an extreme one, it does illustrate the appropriateness differentiating between tasks for which it makes sense to rely on teachers to provide the training and those for which technology can be used to enable students to learn in a self-service mode.

Consistent with a conception of a growing reliance on technology in the schools, in 1982 California set up a $9.9 million technology program that established 15 regional computer demonstration centers where teachers can see and try out microequipment and educational software and obtain training in its use. California also passed a bill that authorizes the expenditure of state funds to disseminate state-of-the-art educational technology.

The third alternative to strict reliance on inservice strategies is telecommunicated instruction, which involves leveraging the amount of instruction that the existing supply of technical personnel can provide. Due to the central importance of telecommunications, this option will be discussed separately later in this chapter.

Clearly, these proposed alternatives to the traditional inservice approach are not likely to receive the political support of the established educational interest groups. Teacher unions in particular are likely to oppose programs that do not channel the majority of the funds to their members. The only way the alternative proposals would be poltically viable is if rising public perceptions of the inability of the public schools to provide emerging skills leads to a coalition of parents and industry groups committed to legislatively imposing cost-effective proposals on the establishment. Such attempts may start occurring around 1985-87 and could signal the last attempt to use political activism to influence the direction of public education. If this attempt fails to overcome the expected resistance of established groups to new forms of delivery systems in education, environmental collapse will probably take over.

The California case is illustrative of how established groups can be expected to react to proposals to increase reliance on the use of technology. The technology program was essentially initiated and lobbied by the governor's office. The position of the California department of education can best be described as benign neglect, since the state superintendent chose to focus on traditional political bread-and-butter issues. Once the program was funded, however, the traditional interest groups rallied to try to obtain a piece of the action and began to discover overnight technology experts in their midst. Since the program was initiated by the governor rather than as a response to grass-roots political pressures, care had to be taken not to upset the traditional interests. Indeed, the bill was not really promoted as the use of technology to deliver aspects of instruction, but rather to develop the capability among teachers to train students to use technology. In addition, the program allocated a portion of the funds to pay teachers to participate in technology workshops.

It remains to be seen, however, whether more radical technology bills—ones that support the use of low-leverage delivery systems—will become politically viable. Also uncertain is whether more creative solutions to the problem of inadequate technical staff, such as the proposed teacher assistant and teacher corps programs, will become politically viable. What is clear is that alternative, nontraditional strategies do exist, and that by opposing attempts to experiment with them, the established public school interests may be sealing their long-term fate.

4. DISSEMINATING INFORMATION

A major problem facing districts seeking to become technologically relevant is obtaining appropriate advice and assistance. There are some grass-roots information dissemination activities available to teachers in the form of technology journals and computer use groups, but currently there are no real vehicles for disseminating such information to decision makers. In particular, there is a need to disseminate information on how to plan for technology acquisition and utilization, as well as how to identify quality software. There is also a need for data bases that maintain information on what software is available for particular instructional and administrative objectives, along with ratings for the existing programs. Finally, there is a need to provide training to assist teachers and administrators to use quality software in school settings.

States can do a number of things to help disseminate the above types of information. Several states, including Colorado and Florida, have funded consultant positions for technology in their respective state departments. Unfortunately, states seldom allocate funds to provide consultants with state-of-the-art software for the workshops they organize. As a result, such consultants usually depend on vendor contributions or sales representatives. While this saves the state some funds and the trouble of determining which of the available alternatives should be purchased for demonstration purposes, it fails to provide districts with the information they really need about quality software. Failure to provide an appropriation for software limits the autonomy of the consultants and puts them in the position of showing the materials of the vendors who are most generous with their contributions as opposed to those who produce the best.

A comprehensive software data base can be maintained on an individual state basis. For example, California has designated the San Mateo county office as a repository of information about software. What probably makes more sense, however, is for a consortium of states to establish a regional or national data base of software ratings. Access to such a data base could be provided on some commercial electronic utility or through a specialized network, such as that provided to forty state agencies through project BEST, which was initiated by the American Council of Educational Technology. Regardless of the particular course chosen, if the data base is to be of value to decision makers it must do more than simply list available programs and must provide critical evaluations of the quality of software packages.

A cost-effective way to establish a statewide training capability is to establish technology labs at several state institutions. Establishing such a lab costs approximately $35,000 to $50,000 for the initial hardware and software and about $20,000 per year in ongoing costs for supplies, maintenance, and updating equipment and software. Setting up two to four such labs in colleges of education would provide facilities not only for preservice but also for inservice training. In return for such investment, however, the state should expect the institution to undertake responsibility for staffing the center out of its existing budget and to require all prospective teachers to do coursework in the use of the technology. In order to be eligible to receive such funds, institutions should be required to compete by submitting plans. The plans should specify how the center will be staffed as well as the extent of the institution's commitment to provide training in technology use skills and to require such skills for graduation. While few institutions have faculty capable of teaching technology courses, good professors can (if they wish) develop acceptable levels of competence in this area with one or two years of effort.

5. ACCOUNTING AND BUDGETARY PROCEDURE REFORMS

If districts are to meet the challenges of changing technology in the absence of massive amounts of new funding, some changes in expenditure patterns will be necessary. While the expenditure shifts required are not large in terms of overall percentages of existing budgets, some changes in accounting and budgetary procedures are needed to facilitate districts making such shifts. The needed changes include (a) promoting greater equity in capital outlay expenditures on a statewide basis, (b) allowing districts to accumulate surpluses, (c) allowing districts to charge for depreciation costs, and (d) allowing, or providing incentives for, districts to use a percentage of general operations for capital outlay purposes.

These changes are necessary because there is no tradition for managing rapidly obsolescing technology in education—or in the public sector in general. The major capital acquisitions (such as buildings, bridges, and motor vehicles) tend to have life spans of eight to eighty years. Given the state of this nation's crumbling public capital stock, one can readily conclude that there are major shortcomings in existing budgetary and management policies with respect to capital assets. Hofman and Cook (1982) estimate that 756 of the larger urban areas will have to spend $100 billion over the next two decades to keep their water systems operable, and that 40 percent of the bridges in the United States have seriously deteriorated. Such neglect of the public capital stock reveals management deficiencies that can be expected to be magnified when applied to rapidly depreciating high-tech capital assets such as computers. Indeed, the application of life-cycle costing techniques with artificially high payoff periods has resulted in the federal government (the largest use of computers) acquiring a largely obsolete stock of computers that are, on average, five years older than their counterparts in the private sector.

These data suggest two problems with existing policy and management biases and techniques. The first is the inability to distinguish between categories of capital assets with differential depreciation rates, such as a computer and a piece of furniture. The second is a gradual shifting of public resources away from investing public funds in the capital assets and capital replacement needed to arrest the effects of depreciation on long-term assets. The trend toward underinvestment in capital assets seems to have occurred at all levels of government. While the federal budget does not separate out capital and noncapital costs, Hofman and Cook (1982) estimate that investment (measured in constant dollars) in public capital declined by 30 percent from 1965 to 1980. It is also not unusual to find school districts where the personnel costs constitute 85 to 90 percent of the budget—a much higher percentage than during the sixties. Although some would argue that the capital expenditure rates of the sixties were artificially high because of the need to construct large numbers of classrooms for the baby boom generation, the trend of reduced allocation to capital outlay is a long-standing one. According to Grant and Eiden (1981), capital outlay expenditures declined from 16 percent of educational expenditures in 1929-30 to 6.7 percent in 1979-80.

While much of the deemphasis on capital expenditures derives from normative judgments and changing political realities with respect to public employee unions, it also reflects management pathologies and governance procedures that prevent adequate levels of capital investment. If schools are to become technologically relevant, not only must they solve the already discussed personnel problems, but many of the state-imposed disincentives for adequate levels of capital investment must also be eliminated. While it may seem impossible and contradictory to upgrade personnel skills while increasing levels of capital investment, that is indeed the primary challenge changing technology poses for both the public and the private sector. Since the private sector faces the same problem, there is not likely to be much public sympathy if education fails to make such an adjustment.

If schools are going to make the kinds of capital investments needed to acquire technology, a number of monetary traditions need to be changed at both the local and the state level. The first is the tendency to ignore capital outlay needs when states develop equalization plans. According to unpublished data compiled by the staff of the Education Commission of the States, only eighteen states had an equalization plan (including full-state assumption plans) to help districts meet capital and debt service needs in 1981, whereas virtually every state provided some form of equalizing state assistance in 1981 for the general operations portion of the budget (however, the degree of equalization varies substantially across the states). Failure to provide more equalized state assistance for capital outlay costs will significantly impair the ability of poor districts to acquire needed technology and expertise.

Another counterproductive practice is the reluctance of most states to allow districts to accumulate surpluses. A budget surplus tends to be viewed as evidence that the school district is sponging local taxpayers for more revenue than it needs. The development of a surplus is therefore viewed as evidence of either incompetent planning or unwarranted demands on the part of district administrators. As a consequence, many states prohibit districts from accumulating surpluses and require either that all revenues be spent in the year they are collected or that all surpluses be returned to taxpayers the following year in the form of reduced tax rates.

The basic assumption behind the restriction on surpluses is that all capital needs can be met from current revenue or the sale of bonds. The work of Young (1982), however, suggests that public agencies employing extensive amounts of high-tech equipment cannot meet capital outlay needs through such sources. While the research was performed on nonprofit hospitals, the results are equally applicable to schools, particularly at present, when it is difficult to convince taxpayers to pass school bonds or increase their tax rates.

Salmon and Thomas (1981) point to another common philosophical argument against allowing surpluses to accumulate: that such a practice violates the "benefit-received" principle. In other words, allowing a surplus to accumulate in effect means that taxpayers are required to pay taxes to support future acquisitions from which they may be unable to reap benefits, since they may no longer be living in the district. Such an argument, however, violates one of the basic rationales for public support of education, what is commonly referred to as spillover benefits.

Spillovers are benefits accruing to individuals in a community other than the one bearing the costs that made the delivery of benefits possible. Since the benefits of education frequently cross regional boundaries and are often passed along indirectly to nonrecepients of the service (i.e., individuals who do not have children in school), all members of each community are asked to support educational services. To exempt capital expenditures from the spillover rationale and thereby demand that only those benefiting directly from such expenditures should be asked to make them does not seem philosophically valid. For example, students who develop skills using equipment purchased from a surplus, to which individuals no longer residing in the district contributed, may find themselves one day using these skills to provide a service to the same former residents in their new locale. Moreover, individuals who leave the community may also derive direct benefits from the surplus, even if they leave before it is spent. For example, if a surplus is essential to maintain quality of services that depend on the use of technology, and the maintenance of such quality is viewed as desirable, individuals moving out of the community can probably obtain a higher price for the sale of their home than they would otherwise get if the quality of the public schools in the community were perceived as eroding.

It appears, therefore, that arguments in favor of allowing (or even stimulating) districts to accumulate surpluses to keep up with changing technology outweigh those against such a policy. There are also a number of policy approaches available to states to facilitate the development of district surpluses. The first and most obvious is simply to make it legal for districts to accumulate surpluses. Such an approach, by itself, would probably be insufficient, given existing political realities, to encourage more than a handful of rich districts to establish such surpluses. Incentives would probably also be necessary.

There are a number of ways that states can motivate districts to develop the surpluses needed to adjust to changing technology. Such a fund could be established by state laws allowing districts to charge a slightly higher tax rate than they could otherwise under either state or taxpayer-approved spending or taxing limitations. The amount of additional tax should probably be specified as a function of a given district's available wealth and prior investment in technology. Young (1982) suggests formulas for determining how much of a surplus is appropriate for a given nonprofit's level of capital investment.

A more direct route to producing surpluses would be to reverse present policy on depreciation accounting. Almost without exception, states do not recognize depreciation as a real cost of providing services. The prevailing argument is that depreciation accounting is appropriate only for profit-making organizations. Although it is true that depreciation charges increase profits in private enterprises, that is a means, not an end. The end is to ensure an availability of funds to renovate existing assets and to reinvest in new and more efficient capital assets—a goal that is equally relevant to education. The issue is not whether a profit is involved but whether rapidly obsolescing technology is involved in the delivery of a service.

Reflecting existing biases against recognizing depreciation costs, most early studies of costs in the area of vocational education (where most instruction-related capital assets are currently concentrated), such as Corazzini's (1966) study, either ignored depreciation or distributed such costs equally among all programs. Unfortunately, such practices do not reflect reality. For example, Keene (1963) found that including depreciation increased cost differentials by 18 percent. Hale et al. (1975) found that including depreciation increased the real cost of vocational programs anywhere from 2 to 96 percent, depending on the type of program. Continued failure to recognize these differences in depreciation costs grossly distorts the actual financial condition of school operations and provides direct incentives for programs with high depreciation costs artificially to extend the life of equipment beyond that which is programmatically desirable.

The result of a failure to recognize and fund depreciation costs can be clearly seen in higher education, where (as already discussed) it has been estimated by the joint DOE-NSF task force (1980) that engineering schools underinvested in capital assets by as much as $700 million during the past decade while continuing to rely on obsolete equipment. The problem of replacing obsolete (although still usable) equipment is starting to have an effect at the community college level, where the capital stock is starting to age. As elementary-secondary schools begin to increase their investment in computers and other forms of technology, a major crunch in technology replacement costs can be expected to hit in four to five years. One can already observe administrators viewing technology as a one-time investment. Indeed, hard-pressed administrators find it so difficult to find funds to *begin* technology acquisition efforts that virtually no planning is done for funding technology replacement.

Describing specific approaches to formalizing depreciation costs in accounting procedures and determining how these costs should be financed are beyond the scope of this book. Several basic operating principles, however, are evident:

(a) Depreciation cost differentials should be recognized in developing program weighting ratios in state finance formulas.
(b) Procedures for obtaining state approval and funding for capital outlay projects should incorporate realistic life expectancies for technology that go beyond estimates of physical survival and also consider degrees of obsolescence.
(c) Whatever surplus funds are generated by depreciation accounting should be restricted to technology replacement use.

Surpluses can help districts update their existing technologies, but there is also a need to help districts make the necessary initial investments to establish such programs. Given the erosion in the amount of funds districts allocate to capital acquisition as a percentage of their budgets, states should allow districts to shift a certain, limited percentage of their maintenance and operations (M & O) budget to capital acquisition for a specified period of time. According to data compiled by the Education Commission of the States (1982), Kansas is the only state that currently permits such a shift. In order to avoid potential abuse, such expenditures should probably be limited to the acquisition of technology. This is particularly necessary in states with low cutoffs for determining whether a purchase is a supplies or capital outlay. For example, in a state that defines capital outlay as the acquisition of a multiyear use asset costing over $2,500, all computer and software expenditures would be defined as materials and would be paid for out of M & O funds anyway. The major problem occurs in poor districts in states without capital outlay equalization plans, and in which the state defines a capital expenditure as a low-cost asset. For example, it is unlikely that poor districts in a state requiring all materials costing more than $100 (which would include all computers and most software) to be paid for out of capital outlay funds will be able to develop a comprehensive program of technology use.

In addition to, or instead of, allowing districts to shift a certain amount of funds from M & O to capital acquisition, states should either raise the standard defining what constitutes capital outlay or at least give districts the option of purchasing computers or software from either source. *Under no circumstances should states follow the lead of those few states that allow districts to shift funds from the capital portion of the budget to M & O.* This can only serve to make it more difficult for districts to reverse the historical trend of inadequate levels of capital investment. An alternative approach to stimulating adequate levels of capital outlay investment is to set a cap on the maximum percentage of the overall budget that can be spent on operations (unless no capital needs can be shown).

The changes in financing and accounting that have been suggested in this section do not guarantee that districts will be able to adapt to the requirements imposed by changing technology. Nonetheless, they can remove existing impediments and increase the opportunity for districts to do so.

6. CERTIFICATION REQUIREMENTS

At one level it seems ludicrous to establish minimum standards of competency in the use of a device such as the computer, for which 70 to 90 percent of all the units ever sold have been in use for less than two years. The society at large is still in the process of discovering what the potential uses of computer technology really are, and which of the available uses are really desirable. Nevertheless, there is a series of uses whose cost-effectiveness has already been documented and which can benefit education. It is therefore important that states stimulate practitioner competencies, so that schools can take advantage of desirable uses of the technology that are already available without locking themselves into a future inability to recognize and take advantage of new uses as they are discovered.

What are the minimum technology-related competencies states should expect and demand from practitioners? The key competencies that teachers need are (a) the ability to evaluate the quality of instructional software, (b) the ability to use a wide variety of existing programs, and (c) some understanding of how to integrate computer-delivered instruction into the overall educational process. The key competencies that administrators need are (a) the ability to structure a process for making decisions about computer acquisitions and (b) the ability to use computers to reduce paperwork. The key to implementing the latter objective is to require that building-level administrators know how to use a data base and word processing programs. Central office administrators should be required to know how to use computerized worksheet programs, such as Visicalc (for financial planning), in addition to the other two types of programs.

The emphasis in most computer-literacy programs to date seems to be on programming. The other common trend is to go in the opposite direction of technical sophistication, requiring only that individuals be able to turn on a computer and regurgitate some information about computers on a test. The major rationales for viewing programming as a key basic skill appears to be tradition (i.e., existing technologists have always considered programming to be fundamental) and the belief that teachers can and should develop their own software. The latter belief is simply not realistic, and its promotion can serve only to stimulate underinvestment in the acquisition of quality educational software by school districts and to generate large amounts of bad, home-brewed software. The typical practitioner does not need to know how to program to use computers effectively. Programming should be a skill required only of those who plan to teach programming or secondary-level mathematics.

7. TELECOMMUNICATIONS POLICY

The computer will, by itself, have a substantial impact on the way we work and play, but it is the mating of the computer and the rapidly changing communication technologies that will have the most dramatic affect on the information economy. It is this combination that is making it possible to distribute and use information in more efficient and convenient forms. It is a highly synergistic combination. However, while telecommunications is advancing rapidly in its own right, educators know even less about this technology than they do about computers. Tucker (in publication) has begun to address the policy issues raised for higher education by the new telecommunication capabilities, but there is no equivalent work at the elementary-secondary level. Nor do most educators (at the elementary-secondary level) have any idea of how the advantages of interactive telecommunications to the consumer and the private sector can also be harnessed in education.

Telecommunications can benefit education in three ways. First, it provides an alternative for exchanging and distributing information. In this category of use, teleconferencing and access to information utilities would probably provide greater benefits during this decade than electronic mail. In addition to reducing the need to travel to obtain information, teleconferencing provides a way to network scarce human resources. Several professional associations and the Department of Education have experimented with national or regional teleconferences, particularly on the subject of technology. One of the major goals of the Association for Educational Communication and Technology's Project BEST, conducted under a grant from the Department of Education, was to start familiarizing educators with teleconferencing. The desire for "high touch" (Naisbitt, 1982)—i.e., the desire for human interaction—will probably limit the appeal and use of teleconferencing in education, however.

The most likely candidates for widespread utilization among the options for information dissemination are speciality electronic data bases. The ERIC clearinghouses are the most widespread examples of such an application in education. ERIC, however, is a limited application. Immediate on-site electronic scanning of the data base is not available (an individual must go to a central site, such as a library or a state department), and only a limited type of material is available (e.g., journal articles are not stored). The first factor limits the service's convenience, and the second, its utility. A more promising approach is the use of electronic data banks that are being established by some of the professional associations and publications. At this time, however, cost factors tend to restrict direct access to these sources to a few locations in a state. Hence, although these newer electronic data bases provide information that is more closely linked to the needs of practitioners, no improvements have been made in convenience and flexibility of access.

Will educators take advantage of an electronic data base if its use is cost-effective and convenient? The answer, judging from the one success story, appears to be yes—at least for certain uses. The success story is the Guidance Information System data bank, which is used widely in secondary schools in the United States. Students typically use this data base in an interactive mode to obtain information relevant to their choice of colleges and careers. Large districts often have the data bank on their own central computer, while smaller districts typically link up to a remote system. That schools are using electronic data bases for guidance functions does not, of course, mean that administrators or teachers would use such a capability to seek information that could help them improve the quality of their work. Nevertheless, the extensive acceptance of this technology is quite striking.

The second way telecommunications can be used in education is to enrich the traditional curriculum. Providing students the ability to access regional, national, and international data banks makes it possible to integrate a new set of appropriate experiences into the ongoing curriculum. The appropriate use of such a capability would be to provide activities in the "computer use skills" and "reinforcement" categories of technology use in Tables 8 and 9. The former category would consist of a form of consumer education in which students would learn the search techniques associated with computerized scanning of such data bases. The latter would consist of providing students in social studies and journalism classes with the opportunity to synthesize information from around the world, even before it appears in the local papers. In addition, the availability of such a capability would be one way to provide activities that can help students improve their higher-order skills in information synthesis and critique. Until research can document the effectiveness of such use, however, there will be no rationale for underwriting the cost of providing *extensive* access time for each student. There could, however, be some future cost-effectiveness rationale if an appropriate data bank were developed for magazine articles, which would enable schools to reduce the cost of periodical subscriptions.

States can provide some assistance in this application by negotiating special discount rates for their schools. Until recently, Source provided a discount for educational uses, but it has discontinued the practice. If information dissemination activities focusing on the potential uses of data bases were successful in increasing the demand for such services, states would then have a much stronger bargaining position from which to press for discounts. Currently states have no rationale for subsidizing use of commercial data bases.

The third and possibly most important benefit that telecommunications can provide for education is a way to leverage available teachers in subject areas where there are teacher shortages, and to provide small numbers of students specialized classes that otherwise would not be fiscally prudent. As already discussed, schools are facing critical teacher shortages in math and science, shortages that are unlikely to be corrected strictly by conventional means. At the same time, declining enrollment is reducing the class size in the advanced courses of many subjects. Given districts' reluctance to close schools unless it is absolutely essential, students' reluctance to leave their school to take classes at another one (a reluctance usually shared by parents), and the cost of busing them even if they are willing to travel, districts are increasingly forced to consider dropping advanced courses.

Telecommunications is potentially an ideal tool for providing quality instruction when there are both teacher and student shortages. *Quality education* (equivalent to the concept of a low-leverage delivery system) is herein used to refer to a situation in which the pupil-teacher ratio in the telecommunicated instructional environment is being maintained at roughly the same level as in the regular classroom. In addition, there would need to be a two-way capability for the two communication modes of video and sound. More highly leveraged telecommunicated instructional environments are, of course also feasible and would clearly be cheaper. It would also be cheaper to rely on one-way communication systems or two-way networks with only one mode of communication. For the purpose of this section, however, let's consider a situation in which the opportunity for interaction and feedback is the same as it would be in a regular class.

Two types of quality telecommunicated environments will be considered. The first is the single teacher; the second is the team-teaching mode (the team consisting of a single teacher and a group of teaching assistants). An example of the first case would be a situation in which a school district has five schools, in each of which seven students are registered for a series of advanced courses. Total enrollment in each of the advanced courses would therefore be thirty-five students—the equivalent of a single class. In this situation a classroom in each school can be equipped to receive and transmit audio and video signals over a communication link between the schools. The teacher would be located in one of the schools, and the other classes would be staffed by aides. Students at the remote sites would be able to interject their questions or comments during the period much as in a regular class.

The second type of telecommunicated environment would occur with several full classes at a number of sites but only one teacher with appropriate skills. In this situation, a team-teaching approach, combining the single teacher with aides at the remote classrooms, would be an option. The teacher would spend part of the period presenting information over the network and student assistants would take over local instruction for the remainder of the period. Each teacher assistant would also be responsible for the clerical duties related to his or her class. If this arrangement seems to resemble the way universities handle large sections of a class, the resemblance is intended.

What would be required to make such a telecommunicated instructional environment feasible? First, legal codes would have to be changed to allow the types of staffing patterns that would be needed. The second requirement relates to the technology itself. Transmitting video images requires sophisticated broadband network capabilities, such as those of coaxial cable, optical fibers, and microwaves (but not voice-grade phone lines).

States have several options for helping districts acquire such capabilities. They can build schools into existing state broadband networks. In a number of states such statewide networks are already in place to support communications for a number of public services (usually police and other emergency services). States can subsidize the expansion of such networks to link schools. The rationale for such subsidies would be that they could ultimately reduce the overall cost of education. Cost-benefit analyses would be required to determine whether potential savings would be sufficient to justify the costs.

A more widespread opportunity for most districts is to try to hook into community cable systems and obtain dedicated use of several channels to provide telecommunicated instruction between schools and between schools and homes. The least costly way to do this is to negotiate such services as part of the bidding process for a community cable system. This requires that school administrators understand the importance of linking into the cable system and be able to convince community leaders and the general public of the importance of incurring the additional expense. It also requires that the bidding cable companies provide such capabilities. In general, large communities get more bidders for a cable system and therefore have more leverage in extracting such concessions.

In addition to disseminating information to increase awareness among local districts of the importance of gaining access to and dedicated use of community cable systems, there are additional opportunities for state assistance. One important service states can provide is to help form consortia of small communities to organize joint bids for a common cable system. The goal would be to create larger systems and thereby increase the willingness of potential bidders to include educational links and channels in their bid.

For communities with established cable systems in which provisions for educational use are not included (particularly when the franchise is not coming up for renewal in the near future), a different approach must be taken. In this case, linking the schools into the existing cable system would involve additional cost to the community. The policy questions then become (a) Should the cost be allowed or encouraged? (b) Who should pay the cost? and (c) How should the cost be paid? Again, there are a number of possible approaches. At one level, state statutes should be examined to make sure that there is no prohibition against using available local and state capital funds to acquire cable networking. At another level, a case might be made for limited state subsidies on the basis of long-term cost savings. It is also important to consider allowing funding for educational cable networking to be obtained via a special add-on property tax or by having a surcharge or municipal tax added to the cable company's subscription fee. This would, in effect, spread the cost of educational networking across all the members of the community who are part of the cable system.

The question of networking cost is a difficult one to address. Tucker (in publication) notes that there are currently a number of communications regulatory issues that will have dramatic impact on the future costs of telecommunications. Since court decisions have made it unlikely that it is legal to require that cable companies provide free educational capabilities on a national basis, the cost to educators will be directly related to the costs for everyone else. Given the complexity of the regulatory issues, it is important that regional conferences and joint state lobbying efforts be organized to push for national policies that are most likely to keep telecommunication costs as low as possible.

The key to making telecommunicated instruction work is the network. It is the knowledge highway. Ritter (1982) estimates that once the networking capability is in place, the cost of equipping a classroom for delivering and/or receiving instruction is only about $6,000. Unfortunately, the tremendous potential of telecommunications is somewhat shrouded by the rapid rate of technological change and dampened by the difficulty of getting a good handle on the policy implications. It is clear, however, that the potential is such that educators need to become more aggressive in trying to get a piece of the action. If states have to make a choice between subsidizing some aspect of computer use, telecommunications should rate right behind software in priority.

8. SUMMARY OF POLICY RECOMMENDATIONS

This chapter has ranged across a wide variety of policy issues. Many of the commonly proposed state policy initiatives for dealing with technology-related problems, such as differential pay and inservice for the problem of inadequate numbers of technical staff, were analyzed and found wanting. This does not mean that they should not be pursued, only that it would be a mistake to place great reliance on them. For example, it was recommended that career differential programs, telecommunicated instruction, and automated instruction must be incorporated into programs to solve the emerging staffing problems. Tables 13 and 14 contain basic suggestions as to the relative priority of each.

Most of the policy recommendations are nontraditional and are therefore difficult to achieve politically—difficult, but perhaps not impossible. State-level policymakers and educators must begin to make realistic assessments of whether the problems that are now starting to surface can be solved with a series of patchwork solutions or whether they signal the need to change some fundamental ways the work of instruction is performed. Educational work is encountering a new reality in which new types of problems are overwhelming the capabilities provided by existing technologies and procedures, much as industrial technology is losing its competitive edge. Some responsible new directions must be cautiously embarked on. The purpose of this chapter has been to suggest what types of state policies need to be pursued to make some of these new directions feasible from a fiscal and legal perspective.

TABLE 13   Recommendations for Joint State Action

Problem	Information General and Distribution	Funding	Activism
Shortages of highly automated nonintelligent software	Develop recommendations for software standards (top priority)	Fund development of software (low priority)	Lobby publishers for better software (top priority)
	Develop data base on software ratings (top priority)		Blacklist publishers that do not supply quality software (low priority)
	Have regional conferences designed to acquaint state level policymakers with technology issues (top priority)		Negotiate licensing agreements (top priority)
Shortages of technical skills among staff and shortages of technical staff		Regional analysis of telecommunication options and costs for delivering telecommunicated instruction (top priority)	Lobby school and municipal officials to take school system needs into account in setting bidding criteria for municipal cable systems (top priority)

TABLE 14   Recommendations for Individual State Action

Problem	Information Generation and Distribution	Funding	Enabling Legislation
Shortages of highly automated nonintelligent software	Provide information to districts on software quality (top priority)	State tax credits for individuals making software contributions to school (top priority)	Allow textbook funds to be used to acquire software (top priority)
	Negotiate licensing agreements with quality software publishers and disseminate pricing agreements (top priority)	State department capability to disseminate information on software ratings and pricing (top priority)	Allow districts to acquire hardware and software from either operations or capital outlay portion of budget (top priority)
	Help organize regional computer fairs (top priority)	Establish software demonstration centers in universities (top priority)	Allow districts to generate surplus for the purpose of acquiring software (medium priority)
	Disseminate information on successful computer use programs (top priority)	Provide matching funds for districts to acquire software (medium priority)	Allow state departments to negotiate licensing agreements with software publishers (top priority)
Shortages of technical skills among staff and shortages of technical staff	Provide information to college students about the teacher assistance and teacher corps program (high priority if program enacted)	Provide funding for a teaching assistance program either in terms of partial payments to provide incentives or providing free tuition in public institutions of higher education (top priority)	Limit percentage of overall budget that can be allocated to M & O expenses (high priority)
	Disseminate information about software and technology available to provide self-service instruction	Contract for development of software in areas of shortages (low priority)	

(continued)

TABLE 14 (Continued)

Problem	Information Generation and Distribution	Funding	Enabling Legislation
	in technical subjects (low till 1985-87; high thereafter)	Subsidize statewide telecommunications systems or a portion of that part of local cable networks being used to subsidize telecommunicated instructional use (medium priority)	Appropriation to carry out key funding priorities
	Try to convince industry of the problem in order to gain their cooperation and some contributed resources (top priority)		Recognize some components of depreciation costs as operating costs (medium/low priority)
	Disseminate information on how to negotiate with municipal officials, cable and phone companies on telecommunication issues (top priority)		Clear legal obstacles to implementing a teaching assistants and teacher corps program (top priority)
			Establish a teaching assistance and teacher corps program (top priority)
			Change certification requirements to require administrators to know how to use technology to reduce paperwork and to require teachers to know how to evaluate and utilize software (top priority)
			Clear legal obstacles to students taking coursework on a computer (low priority prior to 1985-87; high priority thereafter)
			Clear legal obstacles to differential pay programs (high priority in equalized states; no

 CONCLUSION

THE FUTURE OF EDUCATION cannot be the same as its past. The societal environment in which education functions is about to undergo massive change—change induced by extensive technological substitution. The 1985-87 period is expected to be one in which a series of historically rare events in the environment begins to transform the public's expectations for education. At that point, the shift in the economy away from an industrial base toward an information processing one will be evident to Americans, who will then demand that schools prepare students to participate in the new forms of work. At the same time, the environmental changes will also make it impossible for public education to adapt by using conventional strategies. New competitive pressures will force the private sector to compete for the kinds of talents that are increasingly needed to provide the modified forms of education. New social needs, generated by the displaced forms of work and workers, will continue to constrain the funds available to education.

Not only will traditional methods of curricular reform be insufficient, by themselves, to enable schools to adapt; existing political buffers will not protect the public schools from severe consequences if they fail to reform. The same environmental changes that are threatening the existing structure of education are simultaneously providing

203

new types of delivery systems that will make it easier for new forms of organizations to use technology to deliver educational services in a nontraditional, cost-effective manner. This will increase the potential for dissatisfied clients to bypass the public schools. As a result, the consequence of a failure of the public schools to adapt in appropriate ways to the anticipated surge of external change is not one of political isolation, but rather environmental collapse wherein the societal role of public education is severely diminished.

The basic purpose of this book has been to provide a road map for practitioners, policymakers, and researchers showing how to cope with these circumstances. This road map covers a large area and accepts the reality of constrained fiscal resources. It also views many of the current problems in education—such as shortages of teachers with technical skills, declining standards, outdated curricula, inadequate facilities—as interrelated and a consequence of changes in the environment that are going to accelerate.

The basic message, however, is not one of pessimism, but rather of opportunity. The environmental changes threatening the existing structure are also going to make education an increasingly critical factor in our overall economic growth. In addition, a series of comprehensive policy initiatives, if enacted, will enable education to prepare itself not only to survive the coming crises, but also to emerge in an invigorated form. This book has outlined, on the basis of continued moderate economic growth (i.e., barring unforeseen conditions of depression, economic boom, nuclear war, or other disasters), the kinds of appropriate policy initiatives that need to be implemented over the next several years at the local, state, and federal levels of government.

That is not to say that policymakers are ignorant of the problems and have failed to propose solutions. There is indeed a growing awareness among educators and legislators that something must be done to prepare students to meet the demands that a high-technology society and an information-based economy will place on them. Several state legislatures have already passed technology bills, and other legislation has been introduced at the federal level. Many school districts are simultaneously initiating computer-literacy programs.

Unfortunately, most of the existing and proposed efforts focus only on pieces of the problem and are based on simplistic, short-term, and highly traditional strategies. State-level initiatives, partially reflecting budget problems, tend to focus on upgrading technical training by mandating that it be upgraded and/or by mandating computer literacy. State proposals also tend to address the problem of inadequate staff by encouraging districts to establish differential pay programs or to get themselves adopted by industry, and to mandate computer literacy for teacher trainees. When states and federal initiatives propose new spending programs, they tend to advocate targeting such funds primarily for hardware acquisition and/or inservice training. Local efforts, where they exist, are sporadic and are usually limited to exposing students to examples of computer use. The emphasis is on awareness rather than skill development.

Such proposals may seem reasonable and are politically palatable to established educational interest groups, such as unions and teacher training institutions, but they are not likely to make a difference. For one thing, they view the use of technology as an add-on to an existing curriculum that is not providing the most generalized and necessary skills of all: higher-order skills. The proposals also do not address the issue of where schools are going to find the resources—both time and money—to add to the curriculum at a point when they are having problems staffing existing efforts. Such problems are likely to increase. Adding computer-literacy courses at the same time that math/science courses and requirements are being dropped will likely reduce higher-order skills currently being provided.

Existing proposals are also unrealistic vis-à-vis staffing problems. They are unrealistic in the expectation that education can compete with industry for the needed technical personnel on an economic basis. Even if education could compete, however, many other work-condition factors have led to shortages in technical areas and overall declines in the quality of the existing teacher force (e.g., professional workers at IBM are not assigned bathroom duty). Indeed, it is unlikely that a teacher training model exists that can enable lower-ability teachers to provide more sophisticated learning outcomes? Furthermore, it is unlikely that colleges of education, which have themselves largely become ossified, would be able to provide the needed training or assume leadership responsibilities for designing such models, even if such an approach were feasible.

Even if one accepts the underlying assumption of the technology initiatives to date—that the appropriate response to the demands of technology is to teach about the technology—the proposals do not even deal realistically with the problems of how to deliver technology-derived add-ons to the curriculum. If that underlying assumption is incorrect (as has been argued), and indeed the appropriate response is to increase the degree of higher-order skills among students, then the problems with the traditional curriculum and delivery systems are more pervasive than existing technology initiatives recognize. These problems cannot be solved with pinches and dashes of advocacy and wishful thinking, or even by throwing money around. Conventional approaches, which rely on spending money for inservice, differential pay, hardware, and computer-literacy programs, will benefit only a *few* teachers and very bright students, and *all* the colleges of education, technologists, and computer vendors. The core of any serious proposal must recognize that the magnitude of the problems has outstripped the capabilities of the existing delivery system, which relies almost totally on the dissemination of information and inservice training. If the traditional delivery system is no longer adequate for supporting the changes that must occur under realistic scenarios of the future, the essential question then becomes whether more effective delivery systems can be designed.

The recommendations in this book are geared to specifying what changes in delivery systems are needed to support a comprehensive curricular reform that provides some strengthening and reorientation of math, science, and technical offerings and requirements and that significantly improves higher-order skill acquisition among the vast majority of students. Such reform ensures that students will acquire both the specific and the general skills they need to cope with a rapidly changing economy. However, it can be accomplished only by developing and using modified forms of delivery systems that use computer-based technology (a) to help leverage available expertise, (b) to provide the capability for students to learn portions of the curriculum in a self-service mode, and (c) to stimulate the acquisition of higher-order skills through alternative communication modalities.

The recommendations in Chapters V, VI, and VII therefore focus on policies designed to facilitate the use of nontraditional delivery systems and to integrate their use into the existing educational system. These recommendations emphasize research and development programs to provide the knowledge base needed to determine the appropriate uses and roles of technology in the modified delivery systems, as well as to identify, and ensure the availability of, the software needed to support such use. The goal is to use computer-based technology to extend the curriculum, and to improve learning within the traditional curriculum, in a manner consistent with findings from the traditional educational research disciplines, such as learning theory, socialization, and innovation adoption theory. In addition, technology would be used in conjunction with existing knowledge of school improvement strategies (such as time-on-task analysis and curriculum mapping) to increase the effectiveness and efficiency of the teaching force.

While telecommunication can leverage existing quality staff, it will probably not be sufficient in itself to solve the staffing problems. Since inservice and differential pay programs are unlikely to shift the overall capability and composition of the teaching force significantly, alternative approaches, such as teaching assistant and teacher corps programs, are recommended.

Using computer-based technology to alter delivery systems in education not only influences one's notion of professional practice but also has implications for redefining research practices and teacher training strategies. If teachers will not be teaching all that will be taught in schools, then (a) teacher training institutions do not have to teach teachers to teach everything, either in pre- or inservice programs, and (b) research needs to focus on determining what should be taught via technology, as opposed to teacher intervention, under different conditions of technological opportunity. This suggests a shift in teacher training institutions away from a pure focus on training and toward a combined focus that includes the development of computer-based physical models of curriculum enabling students to learn in a self-service mode. Such a focus requires greater interdisciplinary integration of cognitive psychology, artificial intelligence, and computer science into the curriculum design activities of colleges of education.

Social scientists and policy analysts must also shift the focus of their concerns. The use of technology in the environment and schools generates a whole new set of policy issues. School finance must shift away from a concentration on interdistrict funding disparities to address a wide range of new types of equity issues. These include differential access to training in the use of technology and the schools' failure to utilize technology to extend learning opportunities in cost-effective, if nontraditional, ways. For example, even if interdistrict financing were equalized, small schools would still not be able to offer the same instructional opportunities as larger schools within the same district without the use of telecommunications. As a result, failure to use telecommunications in such a circumstance (particularly under conditions of constrained resources) would render educational opportunity a function of school size—an inequity as philosophically abhorrent as that arising from wealth disparities. In addition, political scientists have to shift their preoccupation with studying interest-group politics to monitoring conditions that could produce, and determine if in fact they are producing, environmental collapse. The best guesstimate (based on the technology assessment in Chapter I) is that in the absence of school reform, environmental collapse will become manifest in the period between 1985-87 and the end of the decade.

Regardless of how valid the recommendations are, major resistance to their implementation can be expected. One problem is the general lack of familiarity on the part of most legislators and educational leaders with the capabilities of the new technologies. Individuals tend to be hesitant to support sweeping change that depends on the use of unfamiliar tools and strategies. The major obstacle to implementing the recommended policies, however, is the likely opposition of many established educational interest groups, such as teacher unions and teacher preparation institutions, who are committed to maintaining the status quo. These organizations can be expected to take political action to oppose the use of available funds for hiring teaching assistants and buying technology. Such organizations would probably fight to spend most new funds on reducing pupil-teacher ratios, increasing salaries, and providing inservice activities. The tendency of politically influential groups to oppose many of the recommendations means that legislators will tend to be reluctant to pursue them actively, even if they realize the futility of adhering to traditional approaches. Indeed, such opposition makes sense in the context of the movements of the sixties and seventies, which fizzled out as quickly as they appeared.

There are, however, reasons to believe that political attitudes and realities may begin to change rather quickly and that support for the nontraditional proposals in this book will become increasingly feasible. As the expected environmental changes manifest themselves, the long-term economic implications of these changes will be as evident to key members of the educational power structure as to everyone outside the profession. While the initial reaction of power structures, be they in the public or the private sector, is to resist massive change, the evidence from the private sector is that the more perceptive members of the power structure overcome their initial reluctance and become willing to engage in bold, nontraditional strategies. What is emerging in the private sector, which has already felt the impact of the environmental changes, is a pattern of winners and losers. The former are those companies whose leadership aggressively adopts appropriate nontraditional strategies and which thereby maintain, or increase, market share. The latter are those who are unwilling or unable to change, even after they see the writing on the wall, and thereby lose market share—often to new, relatively small, players.

There are also many perceptive individuals in the educational power structure. It is, of course, impossible to predict whether sufficient numbers of the educational power structure will be willing or able to adopt nontraditional strategies once the implications of the environmental changes become evident, or whether they will do so in sufficient time to make a difference. Clearly, however, as the signals from the environment intensify, many in the educational power structure will recognize that it is in their long-term interest to support the kinds of changes that will prevent the onset of environmental collapse. There will be many who will let the desire to survive in a modified system supersede their reluctance to support change.

In addition, as technology use spreads throughout the society, grass-roots awareness of its potential educational uses (both inside and outside the profession) will increase. General public awareness of the educational potential of the technology will mean that the power of the traditional education lobbies to oppose nontraditional technology-based recommendations will be severely weakened. Grass-roots awareness within the profession will make it difficult for the leadership to oppose its use without substantial losses of credibility.

While recognition of the teaching potential of technology will clearly occur outside the profession as parents start using the computer for educational purposes in the home, there is also reason to be optimistic that grass-roots support for automating many aspects of instruction will gain support inside the profession simply because of its potential to improve the quality of student-teacher interaction. In classrooms all over this country there are dedicated teachers who are seeking new and better ways to motivate and teach their students. What will happen if and when such teachers became convinced that the appropriate use of the computer can unlock their students' minds and free them to focus on the more creative components of teaching? Under such conditions, will teachers foresake 2 percent of a prospective raise in order to improve the quality of their professional life? I am sure the answer is yes.

There is much that is compelling about the arguments and policy recommendations that have been presented in this book, and there are many who will realize that. It is only a matter of time until practitioners and academicians recognize the immense opportunities that reside in the technologies. That recognition will then be the major selling point.

It will take many forms: It will be recognition on the part of teachers and curriculum developers that there is a totally new modality available to communicate with students. It will be recognition on the part of psychologists that there is a new way to test and apply theories of cognition. It will be recognition on the part of academicians from a wide variety of disciplines that they have a new tool for implementing goals that, while philosophically appealing, were formerly infeasible (much as it took space-age fabric and metal to realize Leonardo DaVinci's dream of putting wings on man). It will be recognition on the part of behavioral scientists that it is now possible to study the effects of a powerful new independent variable on a variety of social processes and outcomes. It will be recognition on the part of administrators that they do not have to do repetitive paperwork. It will be recognition on the part of those who care that the use of technology to alter some traditional practices can really improve education. The sum total of these recognitions will be a potent political force that cannot be suppressed by organizational leaders.

There are thus reasons to believe that nontraditional policies may become politically viable during this decade. It remains to be seen whether a sufficient number of influential educators will change their positions in time. What must be understood is that the situation is not one of controlled choice. Inexorable forces in the environment are taking from educators the option of controlling their destiny. The appropriate term is not "choice" or "interest-group politics," but rather *biological models of survival.* If, like the salmon, educators do not modify their instincts and continue to rush headlong against the current, trying to defy the laws of gravity in highly predictable ways even as the amount of pollution and fishermen increase, then public education will also become an endangered species. In the absence of reformulated approaches, the severe erosion of public education's influence will become evident to political brokers.

Even if sufficient educational interests do come to embrace nontraditional policies during this decade, it is critical that they not simply grasp at the seemingly obvious straws, such as differential pay or industry cooperation schemes, whose only virtue is proximity. The issues are complex, and it is critical that leaders begin to think about the problems, and opportunities, presented by technology in a more sophisticated way than superficial curiosity. When, and if, the necessary political coalition emerges to support voluntary nontraditional change, it is important that professionals choose policies that will work. The public will likely give them only one chance. This book has been devoted to providing guidance on the form such choice should take.

There are those who will seek the solace of rejecting the projections of this book, on the expectation that the trends of the first half of this decade will dominate the second half. Such individuals believe public expectations will continue to focus on basic skills rather than on computer use and higher-order skills—thereby negating most of the rationales that have been put forth for the adoption of nontraditional policies. These individuals would do well, however, to remember the lesson of the seventies. It was unanimously accepted by virtually all forecasters that the trends of experimentation, open space, and "touchy-feelie" exploration that were evident in the late sixties and very early seventies would mark the 1970s as one of the most progressive decades in history. Things changed very quickly. This time the change can be anticipated, and social science-based responses can be developed to avoid repeating the mistakes of previous reform efforts.

Dressing up the use of technology in the garb of all the educational fads of the sixties and seventies by isolating it and creating a new infrastructure (called computer literacy) around its use is to miss the fundamental point of the changing reality: that technology does not represent the emperor's new clothes, but a way out of being restricted to the monarchy of traditional practice. Ousting the monarchy, however, does require that the subjects abandon the professional fictions that (a) good intentions are sufficient and (b) it is possible to continue to improve the functioning of social systems by simply manipulating social technologies (which are the backbone of the traditional delivery system). Even that early marvel of social organization, the hunting group, needed the spear to ensure the survival of the species. Educators should therefore not feel ashamed to admit that they in fact need computer-based technology to help cope with a more complex environment.

This book has thrown down a gauntlet—one born out of respect for education and a desire to be critically honest and realistic. It also contains a measure of naïveté, kindled by an awareness of dawning opportunities. I hope there are those who will accept the challenge. In so doing, they will find the recommendations appropriate for improving education.

APPENDIX A
Cost Estimates for a Computer-Intensive Classroom in 1985

The following is an estimate of the cost over five years of placing ten microcomputers (the equivalent of an Apple, with good graphics capability, color monitor, and hard disk interface) in a classroom networked with a hard disk system and printer. No environmental conditioning or reconstruction is expected to be needed, and the electrical consumption of such equipment should be very small.

10 microcomputers × $600	$ 6,000
Hard disk system (10 MB)	1,800
Dot matrix printer	500
Software	2,000
Supplies $1,000/year	5,000
Installation (labor and cables)	500
Service $300/year	1,500
Miscellaneous $300/year	1,500
Total cost	$18,800

Assume thirty students per class, a five-year life expectancy for the equipment, and no salvage value.

Cost per student per year	$ 125

APPENDIX B
A Microeconomic Model for Determining Appropriate Levels of Technological Substitution

The basic principles of microeconomic research could be used to design a formal model for guiding the research effort needed to determine appropriate uses of technology in a low-leverage setting. The basic structure of such a model would be as follows:

— A series of educational activities are occurring in classrooms, and they are related to a series of learning outcomes (both cognitive and affective).

— Each activity has a series of definable characteristics that are related to a particular learning outcome; e.g., time engaged in, degree of individualization, mode of presentation.

— Each activity characteristic has a function relating it to teacher time and cost.

— Each activity has a technology substitution potential ranging from 0 to 1. This factor reflects the extent to which technology can be used to provide the activity characteristics consistent with the results of effectiveness research and technological opportunity at a given point in time.

— There is a definable cost function for substituting technology for particular activities for different states of technological opportunity.

— Constraints to the model include (a) total time available to teachers in a school day and (b) total funds available per student.

To the extent that microproduction function analysis could link classroom activities to learning, and to the extent that alternative approaches to providing instructional activities could be linked to learning outcomes, then the above model could be used to determine analytically whether there is an optimal level of technological substitution for maximizing effectiveness. If it is not possible to specify the first matrix completely, analysis can still be performed to determine the optimal level of technological substitution for maximizing the amount of time students engage in a predefined set of activities. Such analysis would provide a basis for defining more rigorously how much computer access should be considered appropriate for the purposes of defining equity access and developing policy initiatives.

The foregoing model is, of course, an ambitious one. Its feasibility depends on continued basic research in production function theory, classroom management strategies, teacher incentives, and learning theory. The model does, however, suggest a way to link a multidisciplinary, basic research agenda with a common policy objective.

APPENDIX C
Characteristics of Desirable Software

—Content should be consistent with district educational goals and existing curricular material.

—Content should not glorify violence.

—Students should not be rewarded for, or intimidated by, making mistakes.

—Feedback should be immediate and scores provided to students.

—Students should not be rewarded with intricate graphics everytime they get a correct answer.

—Remediation and reinforcement material should have an interesting fantasy element with appropriate graphics.

—System should have options for levels of difficulty and speed of operation.

—When errors are made, system
  (a) should not crash or freeze
  (b) should provide some clue as to where and why the error was made, or at least provide remediation sequence.

—There should be good documentation.

—Multiple-copy license should be available.

—Backup disk should be provided.

—Hard disk option should be available for instructional programs with student management systems.

—There should be adequate provisions for trading and replacing damaged disks.

—Program should be easy to learn and material should be comprehensive for the purpose intended.

—Program should not emit noise when student enters a wrong number, thereby publicly embarrassing the student.

—A floppy disk program should not have to remain in the disk drive after the program has been loaded into the computer. This allows several computers to work off a single copy of the program.

—There should not be spelling errors in the program.

—Teacher should be able to eliminate graphic and sound reinforcement when they are not needed.

—Speed at which program loads should be considered.

GLOSSARY

Academic Flight: A process in which professors voluntarily leave academia for more lucrative and/or more attractive working conditions in industry.

Access Equity: The distribution of opportunity to acquire the skills necessary to compete for jobs in the information economy.

Appropriate Use of Technology: Computer applications that improve learning outcomes, save personnel time, or reduce costs.

Artificial Intelligence: The capability in computer systems to accept instructions in English and/or can make judgments based on prior experiences.

Automated Instruction: Technology applications that enable students to learn either partially or totally in a self-service mode.

Basic: Programming language.

Capital Outlay: That of a district's budget that is used to pay for equipment and buildings.

Cobol: A programming language used for most business applications.

Computer-Assisted Instruction (CAI): Systems that provide computer-based instructional interactions to students.

Computer Literacy: Familiarity with various aspects of computer use, as well as the societal implications of such use.

Computer-Managed Instruction: Program wherein the computer diagnoses weaknesses, prescribes remediation, and/or keeps track of student progress and objectives mastered.

Conceptual Implementation: The mental state of knowing how to implement a service.

Conflict Matrix: Used in student scheduling programs. Indicates the number of students requesting a particular pair of courses (e.g., English I and Algebra I). Used to determine which courses should not be scheduled at the same time.

Cultural Technology: A technology that is found or used in more than 10 percent of households.

Data Base Management System: Software that makes it easy to file information electronically.

Delivery System: A method of stimulating the adoption and/or utilization of a specific technique in the majority of schools.

Drill and Practice Software: Programs wherein the computer initiates and directs the flow of person-machine interaction.

Efficiency Equity: The extent to which the maximum amount of needed educational activities that can potentially be provided per unit cost is in fact provided. This is a measure of the extent to which appropriate uses of technology are integrated into the instructional process.

Electronic Mail: A process of transmitting messages electronically.

Environmental Collapse: A process wherein a substitute for a service or product that an organization provides becomes available in the environment, resulting in a severe loss of the organization's clients and political influence.

Error Trapping: The ability of a program to sense when an input is erroneous and inform the user of the error at the time of data entry.

Guidance Information System: A data base of information used at the high school to help students identify potential institutions and careers for particular interests and aptitudes.

Hardware: The physical equipment of or associated with the computer.

High-Leverage Delivery Systems: Technology used to provide the vast majority of instructional activities and thereby replace teachers.

High Touch: Increased levels of social contact sought by individuals in a high-technology environment.

Intelligent Computer-Assisted Instruction: Systems that can make judgments on why a student is having trouble understanding a concept and can customize the mode of presentation and remediation. Such software also provides the capability to teach more abstract types of concepts and information than regular CAI.

Logo: A programming language for children.

Low-Leverage Delivery Systems: Technology used to provide some instructional activities and supplement those provided by the teachers.

Maintenance and Operations: That part of a district's budget earmarked for providing an instructional program. This includes the cost of teachers, maintenance, and transportation.

Microcomputer: A small computer in which the processor circuiting circuitry is contained on a single chip. Such computers can be as powerful as the large-scale computers of ten years ago.

Microeconomics: A branch of school improvement research that links learning outputs to the nature and quantity of specific classroom instructional processes, as well as the cost of providing such interaction.

Pascal: Programming language.

Physical Implementation: Actually making a particular service available.

Primary Work Tool: A technology whose use is integral to the performance of at least 25 percent of jobs in society.

Production Functions: Equations that attempt to link instructional inputs, such as teacher experience and expenditures, to learning outcomes.

Programming: A process of preparing instructions that will direct the operation of a computer.

ROM (Read-Only Memory): A chip used in computers that can store instructions which are put in at the factory and which cannot be changed or erased without special equipment.

Smalltalk: A programing language developed by Xerox that simplifies the process of communicating with a computer.

Software: A set of instructions that direct the computer to provide specific types of instructional interactions. These instructions are usually stored on a disk or tape.

Spillover: A situation in which the benefits of a community's investment in education may be partially transferred to another community, as when an individual educated at the expense of one community moves to another to apply skills obtained.

Spreadsheet Program: A type of program that provides the capability to manipulate rows and columns of financial (or other types of numeric) data. Simplifies the preparation of budgets and other types of financial analyses.

Tally Matrix: Used in student scheduling programs. Indicates the number of students requesting each course.

Teaching Assistantship Program: A proposed program wherein college students would be funded to teach math and science courses part-time at the elementary secondary level.

Teacher Corps Program: A proposed program that would allow undergraduate students to teach math and science full-time for two years at a beginning teacher's salary.

Technological Opportunity: The potential of a given technology to deliver a particular service at a desired level of cost. For policy purposes, the cost level should probably be below $200 per pupil.

Technological Reluctance: Characterization of a curriculum that provides the type of skill training needed in the information age.

Technological Assessment: Analysis of the likely future impact of a given technology.

Technology Event: A distinct evolutionary phase in societal utilization of technology.

Teleconferencing: Conducting interactive meetings between groups in different locations using (usually) telecommunicated images and voice.

Teletext: One-way transmission of information to the home via television signals.

Unstructured Software: Programs that enable the individual to initiate the interaction with the computer and to control the direction of the interaction.

Video Disc System: A storage medium that can store very large amounts of combinations of information representing sound, text, graphics, and motion pictures in digital form.

Videotex: Two-way transmissions of information to the home via television signals.

Wideband Communications: Systems that use transmitting mediums, such as microwaves, radio signals, coaxial and fiber optical cables, that are capable of transmitting information at very high speeds.

Word Processing: A type of program that provides the capability to enter and edit text and produce documents electronically.

BIBLIOGRAPHY

Alexander, T. "Teaching Computers the Art of Reason." *Fortune,* May 17, 1982, 106, 82-84. (a)

Alexander, T. "Computers on the Road to Self-Improvement." *Fortune,* June 14, 1982, 106, 148-160. (b)

Anders, G. "Colleges Faltering in Effort to Ease Critical Shortages of Programmers." *Wall Street Journal,* August 25, 1981, CVI, 15.

Averch, H. How Effective Is Schooling? Englewood Cliffs, NJ: Educational Technology Publications, 1974.

Baker, E., Herman, J., & Yeh, J. "Fun and Games: Their Contribution to Basic Skills Instruction in Elementary School." *American Educational Research Journal,* Spring 1981, 18, 83-92.

Bell, D. "The Social Framework of the Information Society." Pp. 111-163 in M. Dertouzos & J. Moses (Eds.), *The Computer Age: A Twenty-Year View.* Cambridge, MA: MIT Press, 1980.

Berliner, D. "Tempest Educare." Pp. 120-135 in P. Peterson & H. Walberg (Eds.), *Research on Teaching.* Berkeley, CA: McCutchen, 1979.

Berman, P., & McLaughlin, M. *Federal Programs Supporting Educational Change, Volume 8: Implementing and Sustaining Innovations.* Santa Monica, CA: Rand Corporation, 1978.

Blood, R., et al. *The New Mexico Principalship Study.* Albuquerque: University of New Mexico, 1978. (Unpublished)

Blundell, G. "Personal Computers in the Eighties." *Byte,* January 1983, 7, 166-182.

Bozeman, W. "Computer-Managed Instruction: State of the Art." *AEDS Journal,* 1979, 12, 117-137.

Bracey, G. "Computers in Education: What the Research Shows." *Electronic Learning,* November/December 1982, 2, 51-54.

Brittner, C., & Lientz, M. *Information Services Environmental Assessment.* Los Angeles: University of California, 1981. (Unpublished)

Brown, B., & Saks, D. "Production Technologies and Resource Allocations within Classrooms and Schools: Theory and Measurement." Pp. 53-117 in

R. Dreeben & A. Thomas (Eds.), *The Analysis of Educational Productivity,* Vol. 1. Cambridge, MA: Ballinger, 1980.

Brown, J., et al. "Computers in a Learning Society." Pp. 289-305 in Hearings before the Subcommittee on Domestic and International Scientific Planning, Analysis and Cooperation, *Computers and the Learning Society.* Government Document 23-0820. Washington, DC: U.S. Government Printing Office, 1977.

Business Week. "Robots Join the Labor Force." June 9, 1980, 2640, 26-73.

Business Week. "Missing Computer Software." September 1, 1980, 2652, 46-53.

Business Week. "Window on the World: The Home Information Revolution." June 29, 1981, 2694, 74-83.

Business Week. "The Speedup in Automation." August 3, 1981, 2699, 58-67.

Business Week. "The Rush to Fill a New Niche." August 17, 1981, 2701, 108.

Bylinsky, G. "Those Smart Young Robots on the Production Line." *Fortune,* December 17, 1979, 100, 90-96.

Carey, J., et al. *Teletext and Public Broadcasting.* New York: Alternate Media Center, New York University, 1980.

Carnoy, M., & Levin, H. "Evaluation of Educational Media: Some Issues." *Instructional Science,* 1975, 4, 381-406.

Cole, B. "Computing to Work." *Interface Age,* August 1981, 6, 94-96.

Corazinni, A. *Vocational Education: A Study of Benefits and Costs.* Princeton, NJ: Princeton University Press, 1966.

Craig, L. "Office Automation at Texas Instruments." Pp. 1-51 in M. Moss (Ed.), *Telecommunications and Productivity.* Reading, MA: Addison-Wesley, 1981.

Dreeben, R., & Thomas, A. (Eds.). *The Analysis of Educational Productivity,* Vol. 1. Cambridge, MA: Ballinger, 1980, 53-117.

Drucker, P. "The Re-Industrialization of America." *Wall Street Journal,* June 13, 1980, CV, 10.

Drucker, P. "Clouds Forming across the Japanese Sun." *Wall Street Journal,* July 13, 1982, CVII, 26.

Duchesneau, T., Cohn, S., & Dutton, J. *A Study of Shoe Manufacturing.* Final Report to the National Science Foundation. Washington, DC: National Science Foundation, 1979.

Dunn, D. "Information Resources and the New Information Technologies: Implications for Public Policy." Pp. 493-507 in *The Five-Year Outlook on Science and Technology,* Vol. 2. Washington, DC: National Science Foundation, 1980.

Dunn, D., & Ray, M. *Local Consumer Information Services.* Stanford, CA: Program in Information Policy, Stanford University, 1979.

Easton, D. *A Systems Analysis of Political Life.* New York: John Wiley, 1965.

Education Commission of the States. "Schools Face Both Reduction in Force and a Shortage of Math Teachers." *Legislative Review,* September 29, 1982, 12, 1-2.

Education USA. "Cable TV in the Schools: A Toy Turning into a Tool?" 1980, 22, 353.

Electronic Education. "No Micro Training Available to Education Majors." September 1982, 2, 19.

Elton, C., & Carey, J. *Implementing Interactive Tele-Communications Services.* New York: Alternate Media Center, New York University, 1980.

Emerick, J., & Peterson, S. *Educational Knowledge Dissemination and Utilization: A Synthesis of Five Recent Studies.* San Francisco: Far West Regional Laboratory, 1978.

Ernst, M. "New Contexts for Productivity Analysis." Pp. 52-67 in M. Moss (Ed.), *Telecommunications and Productivity.* Reading, MA: Addison-Wesley, 1981.

Feller, I., Menzel, D. & Engel, A. *Diffusion of Technology in State Agencies.* University Park: Center for the Study of Science Policy, Pennsylvania State University, 1974.

Fisher, C., et al. *Teaching Behaviors, Academic Learning Time and Student Achievement.* San Francisco: Far West Regional Laboratory, 1978.

Forbes, R. "The Information Society." *The School Administrator,* April 1982, 39, 16-17.

Friedrich, O. "The Robot Revolution." *Time,* December 8, 1980, 116, 72-83.

Friedrich, O. "The Computer Moves In." *Time,* January 3, 1983, 121, 14-24.

Froelich, L. "Robots to the Rescue?" *Datamation,* January 1981, 27, 85-96.

Frohreich, L. "Cost Differentials and the Treatment of Equipment." *Journal of Education Finance,* Summer 1975, 1, 52-70.

Gagne, R. "Developments in Learning Psychology." *Educational Technology,* June 1982, 22, 11-15.

Gagne, R., & White, R. "Memory Structures and Learning Outcomes." *Review of Educational Research,* Spring 1978, 48, 187-222.

Gallese, L. "Joblessness May Soar Because of the Changes in Economy Since 1975." *Wall Street Journal,* July 1, 1980, 1.

Gillespie, R., & Dicaro, D. *Computing and Higher Education: An Accidental Revolution.* Washington, DC: National Science Foundation, 1981.

Ginzberg, E. "The Mechanization of Work." *Scientific American,* September

1982, 247, 67-75.

Giuliano, V. "The Mechanization of Office Work." *Scientific American,* 1982, 247, 149-164.

Glass, G., McGraw, B., & Smith, M. *Meta-Analysis in Social Research.* Beverly Hills, CA: Sage, 1981.

Glass, G., & Smith, M. *Meta-Analysis of Research on the Relationship of Class Size and Achievement.* Boulder, CO: Laboratory for Educational Research, 1978.

Glenn, A., Gregg, D., & Tipple, B. "Using Role-Play Activities to Teach Problem Solving: Three Teaching Strategies." *Simulation & Games,* June 1982, 13, 199-210.

Goldman, R. "Pay Television as a Mode of Distribution for Science Programming." *Journal of Educational Technology Systems,* 1980.

Grant, V., & Eiden, L. *Digest of Educational Statistics, 1981.* Washington, DC: U.S. Government Printing Office, 1981.

Guthrie, J., & Zussman, A. "Teacher Supply and Demand in Mathematics and Science." *Phi Delta Kappan,* September 1982, 64, 28-32.

Hale, J., et al. *The Development and Testing of a Model for Determining the Costs of Vocational Education Programs and Courses.* Gainesville, FL: Institute for Educational Finance, 1975.

Hall, G., & Loucks, S. "A Developmental Model for Determining Whether the Treatment Is Actually Implemented." *American Educational Research Journal,* 1977, 14, 263-276.

Hamblen, J. *Computer Manpower-Supply and Demand by States: Fourth Edition.* St. James, MO: Information Systems Consultants, 1981.

Harnischfeger, A., & Wiley, D. "Determinants of Pupil Opportunity." Pp. 223-266 in R. Dreeben & A. Thomas (Eds.), *The Analysis of Educational Productivity,* Vol. 1. Cambridge, MA: Ballinger, 1980.

Hayes, D., & Birnbaum, D. "Preschoolers' Retention of Televised Events: Is a Picture Worth a Thousand Words?" *Developmental Psychology,* 1980, 16, 410-416.

Hayes, D., Chemeski, B., & Birnbaum, D. "Young Children's Incidental and Intentional Retention of Televised Events." *Developmental Psychology,* 1981, 17, 230-232.

Hayes, R., & Abernathy, W. "Managing Our Way to Economic Decline." *Harvard Business Review,* July/August 1980, 58, 67-77.

Heltz, S., & Turoff, M. *The Network Nation.* Reading, MA: Addison-Wesley, 1978.

Heuston, D. Testimony before the Subcommittee on Science, Research and

Technology, April 2, 3. Government Document 67-2830. Washington, DC: U.S. Government Printing Office, 1980.

Hofman, S., & Cook M. "Crumbling America: Put It in the Budget." *Wall Street Journal,* October 7, 1982, CVII, editorial page.

Hymowitz, C. "Employers Take Over Where Schools Failed to Teach the Basics." *Wall Street Journal,* January 22, 1981, CVI, 1, 14.

International Data Corporation. *Office Automation Case Studies.* Waltham, MA: International Data Corporation, 1980.

Jamison, D., Klees, S., & Wells, S. *The Costs of Educational Media.* Beverly Hills, CA: Sage, 1978.

Jamison, D., Suppes, P., & Wells, S. "The Effectiveness of Alternative Instructional Media: A Survey." *Review of Educational Research,* 1974, 44, 1-67.

Jamison, D., et al. "Cost and Performance of Computer-Assisted Instruction for Education of Disadvantaged Children." Pp. 201-240 in J. Froomkin, D. Jamison, & M. Radner (Eds.), *Education as an Industry.* Cambridge, MA: Ballinger, 1976.

Johansen, R., Vallee, J., & Spangler, K. *Electronic Meetings.* Reading, MA: Addison-Wesley, 1979.

Jonscher, C. "The Economic Role of Telecommunications." Pp. 68-92 in M. Moss (Ed.), *Telecommunications and Productivity.* Reading, MA: Addison-Wesley, 1981.

Kalba, K., & Jakimo, A. *The Content of Electronic Message Systems: An Overview of Information Policy Issues.* Cambridge, MA: Kalba Bowen Associates, Inc., 1980.

Keen, P., & Wagner, G. "DSS: An Executive Mind-Support System." *Datamation,* November 1979.

Keene, T. *Foundation Program Cost Differentials for Community Colleges.* Gainesville: University of Florida, 1963. (Unpublished doctoral dissertation)

Kincaid, H., McEachron, N., & McKinney, D. *Technology in Public Elementary and Secondary Education: A Policy Analysis Perspective.* Menlo Park, CA: Stanford Research Institute, 1974.

Kirst, M., & Garms, W. "Public School Finance in the 1980s." *Education Digest,* 1980, 46, 5-8.

Kirst, M., Tyack, D., & Hansot, E. *Educational Reform: Retrospect and Prospect.* Stanford, CA: Institute for Research on Educational Finance and Governance, Stanford University, 1979.

Knott, J., & Wildavsky, A. "If Dissemination Is the Solution, What Is the

Problem?" *Knowledge: Creation, Diffusion, Utilization,* June 1980, 1, 537-578.

Kozmetsky, G. "Education as an Information System." Pp. 232-248 in R. Dreeben & A. Thomas (Eds.), *The Analysis of Educational Productivity,* Vol. 1. Cambridge, MA: Ballinger, 1980.

Kulick, J., Kulick, C., & Cohen, P. "Effectiveness of Computer-Based College Teaching: A Meta-Analysis of Findings." *Review of Educational Research,* 1980, 50, 525-544.

Kutner, M., & Sherman, J. *Rethinking Federal Education Grants and Intergovernmental Relations.* Washington, DC: School Finance Task Force, 1982. (Unpublished)

Lambright, H. *Adoption and Utilization of Urban Technology.* Syracuse, NY: Syracuse Research Corporation, 1977.

Lancaster, F. *Towards Paperless Information Systems.* New York: Academic Press, 1978.

Landro, L. *Wall Street Journal,* April 21, 1982, CVII.

Leontief, W. "The Distribution of Work and Income." *Scientific American,* September 1982, 247, 188-204.

Levin, H., & Rumberger, R. *The Educational Implications of High Technology.* Project Report 83-A4, February. Stanford, CA: Institute for Research on Educational Finance and Governance, 1983.

Levin, H., & Woo, L. *An Evaluation of the Costs of Computer-Assisted Instruction.* ERIC ED 198794, 1980.

Licklider, J. "Social and Economic Impacts of Information Technology on Education." Pp. 84-113 in Joint Hearings before the Subcommittee on Science, Research and Technology, April 2, 3. Government Document 67-283 0. Washington, DC: U.S. Government Printing Office, 1980.

Lipson, J. "Design and Development of Programs for the Videodisc." *Journal of Educational Technology Systems,* 1980, 9(3), 277-285.

Lu, C. "Information Utilities Conference Surveys the Future." *Infoworld,* April 27, 1981, 331-336.

Lucas, W. "The Federal Role in Telecommunications Applications." Pp. 144-155 in M. Moss (Ed.), *Telecommunications and Productivity.* Reading, MA: Addison-Wesley, 1981.

Lund, R. "Microprocessors and Productivity: Cashing in Our Chips." *Technology Review,* January 1981, 33-44.

Madden, J. "Prospects for Videotex and Teletext." Pp. 255-261 in M. Moss (Ed.), *Telecommunications and Productivity.* Reading, MA: Addison-Wesley, 1981.

Main, J. "Why Engineering Deans Worry a Lot." *Fortune,* January 11, 1982, 84-90. (a)

Main, J. "Work Won't Be the Same Again." *Fortune,* June 28, 1982, 61-65. (b)

Malone, T. *What Makes Things Fun to Learn? A Study of Intrinsically Motivating Computer Games.* Palo Alto, CA: Xerox Research Center, 1981.

Mansfield, E. "Basic Research and Productivity Increase in Manufacturing." *American Economic Review,* December 1980, 70, 863-873.

Market Data Retrieval. *Identifying and Getting Your Share of the School Market for Microcomputers.* Chicago: Market Data Retrieval, 1982.

Markoff, J. "SRI Report Predicts Big Changes for Personal-Computer Market." *InfoWorld,* September 28, 1981, 3, 8.

Martin, E. "What Does a Nation Do If It's Out to Win a Nobel Prize or Two?" *Wall Street Journal,* February 10, 1981, CVI, 1.

Masayoshi, K. "In March of the Robots, Japan's Machines Race Ahead of America's." *Wall Street Journal,* November 11, 1981, CVI, 1, 16.

Miller, T. "Political and Mathematical Perspective on Educational Equity." *American Political Science Review,* 1981, 75, 319-333.

Minsky, T. "Because Teachers Dislike Math Too, A Shortage Arises." *Wall Street Journal,* May 19, 1980, CV, 1, 14.

Molnar, A. "Intelligent Videodisc and the Learning Society." *Journal of Educational Technology Systems,* 1979, 89 (1), 31-40.

Monk, D. "Toward a Multilevel Perspective on the Allocation of Educational Resources." *Review of Educational Research,* 1981, 55, 215-236.

Monthly Labor Review. "Productivity Data." December 1982, 105, 85.

Naisbitt Group. *The Trend Report: Executive Summary,* Vol. 2. Denver: Naisbitt Group, 1981.

Naisbitt, J. *Megatrends.* New York: Warner Books, 1982.

Nans, B., et al. *The Emerging Network Marketplace: An Important New Industry.* Los Angeles: Center for Futures Research, University of Southern California, 1981.

National Center for Education Statistics. *Student Use of Computers in Schools.* Washington, DC: Department of Education, March 20, 1981.

National Science Foundation & Department of Education. *Science and Engineering Education for the 1980s and Beyond.* Washington, DC: National Science Foundation/Department of Education, 1980.

Nilles, J., et al. *A Technology Assessment of Personal Computers, Volume III: Personal Computer Impacts and Policy Issues.* Los Angeles: Office of Interdisciplinary Programs, University of Southern California, 1980.

Nilson, J. "Classroom of the Future." *Microcomputing,* 1981, 5, 36-40.

Norman, C. "The International Stakes in Microelectronics." *Technology Review,* January 1981, 40-43.

Noyce, R. "Microelectronics." *Scientific American,* September 1977, 237, 63-69.

Nulty, P. "Why the Craze Won't Quit." *Fortune,* November 15, 1982, 106, 114-128.

Orlansky, J., & String, J. *Cost Effectiveness of Computer Based Instruction.* Arlington, VA: Institute for Defense Analysis, 1978.

Ouchi, W. *Theory Z.* Reading, MA: Addison-Wesley, 1981.

Papert, S. *Mindstorms: Children, Computers and Powerful Ideas.* New York: Basic Books, 1980.

Pelavin, S. *An Evaluation of the Fund for the Improvement of Postsecondary Education.* NC: NTS Research Corporation, 1979.

Pogrow, S. "A Leap (Logistically Efficient Approach) to State Implementation: A Micro-Technology Based Approach." *AEDS Journal,* Winter 1980, 13, 133-143.

Pogrow, S. "In an Information Economy, Universities and Businesses Compete for Workers." *Chronicle of Higher Education,* 1981, 22, 64.

Pogrow, S. "Micro-Computerizing Your Paperwork." *Electronic Learning,* September 1982, 2, 54-59. (a)

Pogrow, S. "Microcomputerizing Your Paperwork Part II: Scheduling and Attendance Packages." *Electronic Learning,* October 1982, 2, 20-27. (b)

Pogrow, S. "Microcomputerizing Your Paperwork Part III." *Electronic Learning,* November/December 1982, 2, 34-43. (c)

Pogrow, S. "On Technological Relevance and the Survival of U.S. Public Schools." *Phi Delta Kappan,* May 1982, 64, 610-611. (d)

Pogrow, S. "Shifting Policy Analysis and Formation from an Effectiveness to a Cost Perspective." *Education Evaluation and Policy Analysis,* Spring 1983, 5, 75-82.

Porat, M. *The Information Economy: Definition and Measurement.* Washington, DC: Department of Commerce, 1977.

Prince, S. "Information at Your Fingertips." *Electronic Learning,* 1981, 1, 38-41.

Quality Education Data, Inc. *Microcomputer Data.* Denver: Quality Education Data, Inc.

Redfield, D., & Rousseau, E. "A Meta-Analysis of Experimental Research on Teacher Questioning Behavior." *Review of Educational Research,* 1981, 51, 237-245.

Ritter, C. "Two-Way Cable TV: Connecting a Community's Educational Resources." *Electronic Learning,* October 1982, 2, 60-63.

Roy, R. "The Science Establishment Flunks." *Wall Street Journal,* October 8, 1982, CVII, editorial page.

Sabatier, P. "The Acquisition of Technical Information by Administrative Agencies." *Administrative Science Quarterly,* 1978, 23, 396-417.

Salmon, R., & Thomas, S. "Financing Public School Facilities in the 80's." *Journal of Education Finance,* Summer 1981, 7, 88-109.

Schramm, W. *Big Media, Little Media: Tools and Technologies for Instruction.* Beverly Hills, CA: Sage, 1977.

Simon, H. "Designing Organizations for an Information-Rich World." Pp. 37-63 in M. Greenberger (Ed.), *Computers, Communications, and the Public Interest.* Baltimore: Johns Hopkins University Press, 1971.

Simon, H., & Grant, V. *Digest of Educational Statistics, 1971.* Washington, DC: Department of Education, 1972.

Stallings, J. *Implementation and Child Effects of Teaching Practices in Follow-Through Classrooms.* Monograph of the Society for Research in Child Development, 1975.

Strassman, P. "The Office of the Future: Information Management for the New Age." *Technology Review,* December/January 1980, 54-65.

Sternberg, R., & Davidson, J. "The Mind of the Puzzles." *Psychology Today,* June 1982, 16, 37-44.

Summers, A., & Wolfe, B. "Do Schools Make a Difference?" *American Economic Review,* 1977, 17, 639-652.

Tapscott, D. "Investigating the Electronic Office." *Datamation,* March 1982, 28, 130-138.

Thomas, D. "The Effectiveness of Computer-Assisted Instruction in Secondary Schools." *AEDS Journal,* 1979, 12, 103-116.

Tobias, S. "When Do Instructional Methods Make a Difference?" *Educational Researcher,* April 1982, 11, 4-9.

Toffler, A. *The Third Wave.* New York: Bantam, 1980.

Tucker, M. "Policy Implications of Changing Technology." Presented at the Technology and School Improvement Conference, sponsored by the McRel Regional Educational Laboratory, Vail, Colorado, July 27, August 2, 1982. (a)

Tucker, M. *Making Policy for the Information Industry: The Human Resources Bottleneck.* Washington, DC: Project on Information Technology and Education, 1982. (b)

Tucker, M. "The Turning Point: Telecommunications and Higher Education." *Journal of Communication* (in publication).

Tydeman, J. *Videotex: A Dozen Public Policy Concerns and a Design to Understand Them.* Menlo Park, CA: Institute for the Future, June 1980.

Tydeman, J., & Lipinski, H. *T.A. on Teletext/Videotex.* Menlo Park, CA: Institute for the Future, December 1980.

Tyler, M. "Telecommunications and Productivity: The Need and the Opportunity." Pp. 1-51 in M. Moss (Ed.), *Telecommunications and Productivity.* Reading, MA: Addison-Wesley, 1981.

Urrows, E., & Urrows, H. "France Plans 30 Million Terminals for Less Than Cost of Phone Books." *InfoWorld,* September 28, 1981, 3, 50.

U.S. General Accounting Office. *Contracting for Computer Software Development—Serious Problems Require Management Attention to Avoid Wasting Additional Millions.* Washington, DC: U.S. Government Printing Office, 1979.

Uttal, B. "What's Detaining the Office of the Future?" *Fortune,* May 3, 1982, 106, 176-196.

Vance, G., & Eiden, L. *Digest of Educational Statistics, 1981.* Washington, DC: Department of Education, 1981.

Victor, V., & Schlechty, P. "The Distribution of Academic Ability in the Teaching Force." *Phi Delta Kappan,* September 1982, 64, 22-27.

Waldholz, M. "Computer Diagnosis of Medical Cases Gets Mixed Reviews." *Wall Street Journal,* August 19, 1982, CVII, 36.

Walling, V., Thomas, T., & Larson, M. *Educational Implications of In-Home Electronic Technology.* Menlo Park, CA: Stanford Research Institute International, 1979.

Wall Street Journal. "Some Bet Portable Terminals Will Be Next Consumer Rage." June 12, 1981, 27.

Wassily, L. "The Distribution of Work and Income." *Scientific American,* September 1982, 247, 188-204.

Wendling, W., & Cohen, J. *The Relationship of Educational Resources to Student Achievement Levels in New York State.* Denver: Educational Commission of the States, 1980.

Yankee Group. *The Report on Electronic Mail.* Cambridge, MA: Yankee Group, 1979.

Yankee Group. *Personal Computers in the Home.* Cambridge, MA: Yankee Group, 1982.

Yin, R., et al. *Changing Urban Bureaucracies: How New Practices Become Routinized.* Santa Monica, CA: Rand Corporation, 1978.

Young, D. "Nonprofits Need Surplus Too." *Harvard Business Review,* January/February 1982, 60, 124-131.

Yurow, J. (Ed.). *National Information Policy Issues.* Washington, DC: National Telecommunications and Information Agency, Department of Commerce, 1981.

ABOUT THE AUTHOR

Stanley Pogrow is Associate Professor of Educational Administration at the University of Arizona, where he specializes in instructional and administrative uses of computers. The global perspectives in this book reflect his wide variety of work experiences and social science background. He has taught math (grades 7-12) in the New York City Public Schools, worked as a program manager in the California State Department of Education and served as a policy analyst at the National Science Foundation. He has also taught courses in school finance, the politics of education, and organization theory at the University of Illinois at Urbana-Champaign and the University of New Mexico. His specialty at the National Science Foundation was analyzing the implications of research in the fields of technology assessment, and the determinants of technology adoption decisions, for designing federal policies to stimulate increased societal levels of innovation. Dr. Pogrow is a career educator who loves to use computers but hates to write programs. He is also incredibly inept at Pac-Man and Asteroids. Instead, he spends a great deal of time helping districts establish state of the art computer use programs. His primary passion is developing ways to use technology to improve higher-order thinking skills among early elementary students—particularly disadvantaged students. He is currently working with several schools to determine the extent to which the computer can aid in the development of analytical skills.